BIRTHINGS
and
BLESSINGS

II

BIRTHINGS
and
BLESSINGS
II

More Liberating Worship Services
for the Inclusive Church

GAIL ANDERSON RICCIUTI
and
ROSEMARY CATALANO MITCHELL

CROSSROAD • NEW YORK

1993

The Crossroad Publishing Company
370 Lexington Avenue, New York, NY 10017

Library of Congress Cataloging-in-Publication Data

Ricciuti, Gail Anderson.
    Birthings and blessings, II : more liberating worship services for the inclusive church / by Gail Anderson Ricciuti and Rosemary Catalano Mitchell.
      p. cm.
    ISBN 0-8245-1380-0
    1. Women—Prayer-books and devotions—English. 2. Liturgies.
I. Mitchell, Rosemary Catalano. II. Title. III. Title: Birthings and blessings, 2.
BV4844.R53 1993
264'.0082—dc20   93-20569
                                         CIP

Dedicated to the congregation
of
The Downtown United Presbyterian Church,
whose courage is our true inspiration

Contents

7

Part II
Celebrations for Inclusive Communities

Preface

Advent 1992 marked the fifth anniversary of Women, Word, and Song gatherings at the Downtown United Presbyterian Church in Rochester, New York. The services have now become an established part of our church life, with an average attendance of fifty to sixty women at each gathering— including women from a wide range of religious traditions and women who have no church background. Others have shared with us many, many stories of how they left the mainline institutional church and are only now finding their way "back home."

The stories we have heard remind us of our own faith journeys, which begin with baptism. We are reminded that our call to serve the church is indeed the same call as our baptism. Some of our own experiences have caused us to consider joining the exodus from oppressive church structures; but there is a bond that keeps us, thus far, part of the institution. As women of the church we have experienced "the love that will not let us go"; and we have come to understand that this loving bond is covenanted first in the baptism of all believers.

Marjorie Procter-Smith in her book *In Her Own Rite: Constructing Feminist Liturgical Tradition* writes about this persistent calling:

> Images of counterculture or renunciation imply a voluntary move-
> ment to the margins. However, women are already involuntarily
> marginalized in the church... and in the culture. Therefore we do
> not need to move out any farther; if we are to "exodus" it must be
> an exodus out of marginality and into the center: the term "eiso-
> dus" would seem to be a better expression of our claiming the
> center. (147–48)

That is exactly what we have attempted to do these last five years with Women, Word, and Song: to claim the center, to set aside time and space for women to engage in biblical reflection, theological discussion, and liturgical innovation. It has been very exciting, life-giving, and powerful.

In the first volume of *Birthings and Blessings,* we outlined briefly some "foundational assumptions" that guide our work in creating liberating worship experiences. One that bears further expansion, and is influenced by our grounding in the Reformed tradition, is the centrality of the Word. It seems to us that a truly liberating hermeneutic requires an almost rabbinical de-votion, in terms of taking the Word apart piece by piece, "chewing" on it, feasting on it. And an individual, or a community, may do this by means of a holy curiosity: questioning not only *what* it means but also, as the poet

John Ciardi once put it, *how* it means. To engage in this process evidences no disrespect but rather a profound love for, and honoring of, the Word. When experiential engagement is added to an intellectual grasp of the text, enriched understanding is inevitable.

Using Elisabeth Schüssler Fiorenza's principle of a "hermeneutic of suspicion," those who would grow the tree of worship from the seed of a text are freed to be bold in confronting the Word. Scripture is resilient to questioning! Like the oyster, however, it does not give up the pearl easily or obviously. Here, then, are some questions that can begin to carry us from the text to the creation of a worship experience:

- With whom or what do you identify when hearing this Scripture reading? That is, from what vantage point do you approach it? The answer will make a great difference in the insights and worship forms that result. (In Mark 5:24–34, for instance, do you enter the text as the bleeding woman? as Jesus? as someone in the crowd? as one of the disciples? or as a "doctor of the law"? In Jeremiah 18:1–6, do you identify with Jeremiah, watching the vision unfold? Or do you experience the story as if you were the clay in the potter's hand being molded, broken, remolded? Or as the Potter/God, forming the House of Israel at the potter's wheel?)

- What did it mean to those who wrote it and/or to those who heard it — in the context of their culture, social condition, era, history?

- What does it mean *now*, to *us*? As a "secular" culture? As a church? As women? As a minority? As shut-out, alienated, or oppressed? Or as affluent, influential, mainstream, Western, and Anglo? Or as women of color?

- What does the text free us to do? To be?

- What is the Good News — the life-giving word — in this passage? Is there *bad* news here? If so, how do we understand and redeem it?

- What is the specific message of power, healing, mercy, liberation, or comfort contained herein for us as women? And how, specifically, would this differ from its message for the church-in-general, for children and young people, or for *men*?

- What questions does the passage ask, imply, open up, or leave hanging *unanswered* for us to struggle with?

- How could we get a visceral experience of the Word: how does it feel, smell, look, move, sound, taste? How can we embody or image it among us in more than "words, words, words"?

As the reader can see, a text questioned in this manner yields so much "grist for the mill" that the challenge is how to *limit* the focus for a single worship experience! For this reason, we have found that each service in this book could potentially be an entire retreat weekend; and we hope that creative friends will find many ways to expand individual segments for the purpose of deeper nurture and empowerment for their own communities.

Acknowledgments

Many members and friends of the Downtown United Presbyterian Church continue to be a constant source of support and encouragement for our ministry and especially for our Women, Word, and Song gatherings. Those who have contributed in many different ways are Ellie Newell, Rebecca Parks, Martha Brown, Rebecca Seifert, Pat Kulaga, Lynn Lord, Mary Mohlke, Georgiana Prasil, Connie Clay, Susan Riblett, John Holtzclaw, Tom Munn, Herbert Berndt, Barbara Griffis, and Rev. Linda Morgan Clement.

The staff of DUPC has helped us in so many ways. We are especially grateful to Alan Jones, Dr. J. Melvin Butler, Dr. John Bodinger, Jerry Mosholder, Hanson Johnson, and Marybelle Davidson.

The spirit of this community is wonderfully exemplified by Diane Davison-Jannarone, who never said no to even the most outlandish request (such as furnishing two hundred bags of salt). We are especially grateful for her labor of love in researching the alternative hymns for each service.

Suzanne Goodrich has always been graciously willing to devote her gifts wherever needed; and for her friendship-in-action we are most appreciative.

We are deeply grateful to our friends Dr. Virginia Ramey Mollenkott and Debra Lynn Morrison, without whose generosity, spiritual encouragement, technical help and loving support this book could never have been realized in the current crucible of our ministry. The Rev. Lillian McCullough Taylor has also been a wonderful source of enthusiastic encouragement in the time since publication of our first volume.

We have been inspired by, and have drawn frequently from, the work of Sr. Miriam Therese Winter; we are indebted to her as one who has travelled ahead of us, pioneering new trails in liturgical renewal for her sisters.

We are able to include the many resources in this book because communities of women in our denomination have provided grants, for which we are most grateful:

- The Women's Concerns Team of the Synod of the Northeast, Presbyterian Church, U.S.A.

- The Community for Reflection and Direction, Justice for Women, The Women's Unit, Presbyterian Church, U.S.A.

- The Theology and Worship Ministry Unit, Presbyterian Church, U.S.A.

Finally, we feel immense appreciation for the skill of John Eagleson, our editor, and for the gift of his partnership with us.

Key for Sources of Suggested Alternate Hymns

HB   *The Hymnbook*. Philadelphia: Presbyterian Church, U.S., Presbyterian Church, U.S.A., and Reformed Church in America, 1955.

HUCC   *The Hymnal of The United Church of Christ*. Philadelphia: United Church Press, 1974.

LBW   *Lutheran Book of Worship*. Philadelphia: Lutheran Church in America, American Lutheran Church, Evangelical Lutheran Church of Canada, Lutheran Church–Missouri Synod, 1978.

MH   *The Methodist Hymnal*. Nashville: Methodist Publishing House, 1964.

PH   *Pilgrim Hymnal*. Boston: The Pilgrim Press, 1931, 1935, 1958.

TPH   *The Presbyterian Hymnal*. Louisville: Westminster/John Knox Press, 1989.

UMH   *The United Methodist Hymnal*. Nashville: Abingdon Press, 1989.

WB   *The Worshipbook*. Philadelphia: Western Press, United Presbyterian Church (U.S.A.), 1970.

NHLC   *New Hymns for the Life of the Church: To Make Our Prayers and Music One*. Music by Carol Doran, words by Thomas H. Troeger. New York: Oxford University Press, 1992.

Suggested Resources for Music

Everflowing Streams. Ruth C. Duck and Michael G. Bausch, eds. New York: Pilgrim Press, 1981.

A Singing Faith, by Jane Parker Huber. Philadelphia: Westminster Press, 1987.

Inclusive Language Hymns (based on *The Pilgrim Hymnal*). The First Congregational Church (Amherst, MA 01002), 1984.

WomanPrayer/WomanSong, by Miriam Therese Winter. Oak Park, Ill: Meyer-Stone Books, 1987; available from Crossroad Publishing Co., 370 Lexington Ave., New York, NY 10017.

Borning Cry: Psalms, Hymns, and Celebrations, vols. 1 and 2, by John Ylvisaker, Inc., Box 321 Waverly, IA 50677.

A Birthings and Blessings Resource Kit is available,
containing the following items:

- Pattern grid for shields for "Daughters of Zelophehad" (see p. 40).
- Sample "kite" bulletin cover for "Catch the Wind" (see p. 66).
- Sample sash for "She with the Flow of Blood" (see p. 75).
- Sample salt bag materials and instructions for "Salted and Holy" (see p. 82).
- Pattern for family tree for "Family Values..." (see p. 91).
- Sheet music (melody line) for the song "For the Fruit of Your Womb" from "Family Values..." (see p. 92).
- Sheet music (melody line) for "Sophia's Song" from "Croning" service (see p. 116).
- Copy-ready samples of Application and Recommendation forms for "The Discipleship Employment Office" (see p. 137).

To order, send name and address, plus $6.00 postage and handling (payable by check or money order) to:

Birthings and Blessings Resource Kit
c/o Diane Davison-Jannarone
Downtown United Presbyterian Church
121 N. Fitzhugh Street
Rochester, NY 14614

Make check payable to: Diane Davison-Jannarone.

PART I

Women, Word, and Song

1

A FEMINIST SERVICE OF LESSONS AND CAROLS

(Advent)

INTRODUCTION

One of the blessings of the Christmas season is the exquisitely beautiful Service of Lessons and Carols broadcast from King's College, Cambridge, England, each year on Christmas Eve. In its quiet beauty and the majesty of its cadence, the flow of "salvation history" is recalled from Genesis through the incarnation of divine Love in the world with the birth of Jesus. *However* (there seems always to be a "however" for feminists of faith!): Upon closer exploration, we realized that the cycle of readings is distressingly biased in a traditional, patriarchal direction. Eve is portrayed as derivative of Adam, the temptress who caused him to sin. Abraham *alone* receives the promise that his seed will multiply into blessing. Other than the "sin of our first mother" and the annunciation to Mary, women are, in fact, primarily invisible in the traditional nine lessons.

Yet it seemed to us that faith communities with a liberating hermeneutic should not be deprived of the beauty and meaning of all that is *good* in the tradition. We also wished to offer a similar experience of reverent reflection in the Advent season for women whose lives become all too hectic in the press of the holidays. The task that presented itself was to re-form the traditional lections into a telling of the biblical story of *liberation,* whose crowning chapter is the coming of the Christ. Using the stories of our sisters in faith, drawn from Scripture and the sacred writings of women both ancient and contemporary, this feminist service of lessons and carols was created. (Note that the eighth reading, "The Wise Women," inspired by Matthew's account of the Magi, was first told by our own community and is the focal piece of the second service in this volume, where its discovery is described; see below p. 31.) The service extends the pattern of the Cambridge cycle by adding prayer responses to each couplet of lessons and carols as a way of opening space for the community to encounter God as more than just "hearers of the Word." The beauty of the resulting worship experience creates the intention among us that such a service be repeated annually to express the in-breaking of God's *new* Day.

PREPARATION

The worship space is set up in circular fashion, with two semicircular banks of chairs facing in toward a round center table covered with a plain white or festive cloth, on which stand nine pillar candles, unlit, of varying heights and sizes — one for each lesson. (Candles are most effective if a single color — white, purple for Advent, or red — is used.)

Votive lights and tapers are arranged in window sills and around the periphery of the room and are burning when worshippers arrive, creating a softened glow. Other lighting in the space is dimmed, remaining only bright enough for participants to see the words of hymns. Readers — who should be supplied with printed copies of their readings — may also be equipped with small penlights to facilitate their task.

❀

OPENING WORDS

> How silently,
> how silently
> the wondrous gift is given.
>
> I would be silent now,
> God,
> and expectant...
>   that I may receive
>   the gift I need,
>   so I may become
>   the gifts others need.
>
> —Ted Loder,
> from *Guerrillas of Grace*[1]

WORDS OF WELCOME

THE FIRST LESSON

READING

From Genesis 1:1–5, 9–12, 16–18, 20–21, 24–27, 31: Original Blessing, in which our destiny is revealed in creation, rather than in curse.

PRAYER RESPONSE

A brief, guided meditation in which worshippers are led to envision the flame of God deep within them, slowly expanding to surround them, and then the light growing to encircle the entire room; and silently to give thanks for the creative and holy image of God Herself in us.

CAROL

"All Beautiful the March of Days," *The Presbyterian Hymnal*

SUGGESTED ALTERNATE HYMNS

"God of the Sparrow" (TPH, UMH)

"God Who Stretched the Spangled Heavens (LBW, TPH, UMH)

"I Sing the Mighty Power of God" (HB, HUCC, MH, PH, TPH, UMH)

THE SECOND LESSON

READING

The God Who Does Not Blame

We see so much evil around us, so much harm done, that we think it impossible that there is any good in this world. We look at this in sorrow and mourn so that we cannot see God as we should.

This is because we use our reason so blindly, so unfully and so simple-mindedly that we are unable to know the marvelous wisdom, capability and goodness of the joyful Trinity.

Just as the joyful Trinity created all things out of nothing, so also this same blessed Trinity will make well all that is not well. . . . Peace and love are always in us, being and working; but we are not always in peace and love. God is ground of our whole life in Love, and wants us to know this. God is also our everlasting keeper and wants us to know this.

God is our friend Who keeps us tenderly while we are in sin, and touches us privately, showing us where we went wrong by the sweet light of compassion and grace, even though we imagine that we will be punished.

I saw no vengeance in God, not for a short time, nor for a long — for as I see it, if God were vengeful, even for a brief moment, we would never have life, place, or being.

In God is endless friendship, space, life, and being.

I know by the common teaching of Holy Church and by my own feeling that the blame for our sins clings to us continually while we are on this earth.

How amazing it was, then, to see our God showing us no more blame than if we were as clean and whole as the Angels in heaven!

—Julian of Norwich,
"The God Who Does Not Blame"[2]

PRAYER RESPONSE

This prayer, by another mystic — Hildegard of Bingen — is read by a single voice and need not be printed in the order of worship.

O Holy Spirit,
Fiery Comforter Spirit,
Life of all creatures,
Holy are you,
     you that give existence
     to all form.

Holy are you,
     you that are balm
     for the mortally wounded.

Holy are you,
     you that cleanse deep hurt.

Fire of love,
breath of all holiness,
you are so delicious to our hearts.

You infuse our hearts deeply
with the good smell of virtue.

> —Hildegard of Bingen,
> "O Holy Spirit"[3]

CAROL

"Day is Done," *The Presbyterian Hymnal*

SUGGESTED ALTERNATE HYMNS

"How Firm a Foundation" (HB, HUCC, LBW, MH, PH, TPH, UMH, WB)

"O God of Love, O God of Peace" (HB, HUCC, LBW, PH, TPH)

THE THIRD LESSON

READING

Ruth 1:1–9, 16–17: The Covenant of a Sister. By her promise, a foreign woman takes her place in the lineage of Jesus.

PRAYER RESPONSE

Each worshipper is asked to think of a sister in faith who has made a difference in the course of her own life; and then, when bidden by the leader, all together voice the first names aloud. The leader closes with a simple prayer of thanksgiving for the way God has cared for us through the lives of our sisters.

CAROL

"For Ages Women Hoped and Prayed," words by Jane Parker Huber,
A Singing Faith

SUGGESTED ALTERNATE HYMNS

"If All You Want Lord, Is My Heart" (NHLC)

"Lord Speak to Us, That We May Speak" (LBW, MH, PH, TPH, UMH)

THE FOURTH LESSON

READING

Esther 3:8–11, 4:1–17: A Woman Risks Her Life for Her People

PRAYER RESPONSE

The leader, repeating the words "For such a time as this...," invites each worshipper to turn to another and to share what gift(s) she feels God is "growing" in her for the calling of this age. The leader should note here that conversation-from-the-heart can also be prayer in a profound sense.

CAROL

"Lift Every Voice and Sing," *The Presbyterian Hymnal*

SUGGESTED ALTERNATE HYMNS

"God is My Strength and Salvation" (HB, MH, PH, TPH, WB)

THE FIFTH LESSON

READING

Isaiah 11:1–9: The Peace of Christ's Realm Is Foretold

PRAYER RESPONSE

Using the format of bidding prayers, the community is asked to voice in one word or phrase each:

   a. A place in the world for which they pray for peace,

   b. An arena in our own society that needs Christ's healing advent;

   c. A group of persons (the homeless, AIDS sufferers, etc.) in need of the wholistic peace of Christ.

CAROL

"People, Look East," *The Presbyterian Hymnal*

SUGGESTED ALTERNATE HYMNS

"What Star Is This, with Beams So Bright?" (HUCC, PH, TPH, WB)

THE SIXTH LESSON

THE ANNOUNCEMENT:
WOMEN'S ORDINATION (Luke 1:26–38)

One: Six months after Elizabeth conceived,
the angel Gabriel was sent by God
to the Galilean town of Nazareth,
to a virgin betrothed to a man named Joseph,
and the virgin's name was Mary.
The angel said to Mary:

All: "Shalom, O highly favored one;
God Shaddai is with you!"

One: She was deeply disturbed by these words,
and wondered what they might mean.
The angel said to her,

All: "Mary, do not be afraid,
for God is pleased with you.
Listen closely.
You will conceive and bear a child
and you shall name him Jesus.
He will flourish
and he will be called
the child of God Most High.
And Shaddai will give to Jesus
the authority of leadership,
to preside over the household of God
and all God's people forever."

One: Then Mary said to the angel:
"How will this happen,
for I am a virgin?"

All: "The Holy Spirit will come to you,
the shadow of Shaddai will cover you;
the child you bear will be holy
and will be called the child of God.

> Furthermore, your kinswoman Elizabeth
> in her old age
> has also conceived a son,
> and she who was said to be barren
> is already six months pregnant,
> for nothing is impossible for God."

One: And Mary quietly responded,
"I am one with the will of God;
let it happen as you say."

PRAYER RESPONSE

Mary's Song: A Psalm for Every Woman

Mary: My soul celebrates Shaddai!

All: My spirit sings to Shekinah-Shaddai,

Mary: for She erases my anonymity

All: so that all generations of women are blessed.

Mary: She Who has power to open the womb
has done great things for me.

All: Holy is Her name.

Mary: Her mercy flows
through mother to daughter

All: from generation to generation.

Mary: Her maternal strength
strikes at the roots of evil,
and it departs.

All: She pushes the proud
from the pinnacles of power
and lifts up little people.

Mary: She feeds her hungry daughters,

All: but those who are filled to the brim
with opportunity,
She sends away.

Mary: She soothes all those who turn to Her,
remembering Her compassion,

All: keeping Her promise to Sarah
and Her progeny forever.

—Miriam Therese Winter,
adapted from *WomanWord*[4]

A CAROL FOR LISTENING

"Startled By a Holy Humming," from *New Hymns for the Lectionary*[5]

SUGGESTED ALTERNATE HYMNS

"The First One Ever" (UMH)

"To a Maid Engaged to Joseph" (TPH, UMH)

THE SEVENTH LESSON

READING

Luke 2:1–7: The Birth of Jesus

PRAYER RESPONSE

In this instance the worshippers are invited to sing the carol as a prayer.

CAROL

"In the Bleak Midwinter," *Inclusive Language Hymns*

THE EIGHTH LESSON

READING

"The Wise Women," after the account of Matthew 2:1–18; the text of this story can be found below on p. 32.

PRAYER RESPONSE

Worshippers are led in intercessory prayers, either spoken or silent, for "Rachel and her children" — women and children in need — in diverse situations around the world.

CAROL

"Coventry Carol"

SUGGESTED ALTERNATE HYMNS

"Lions and Oxen Will Feed in the Hay" (NHLC)

"Midnight Stars Make Bright the Sky" (TPH)

"What Child Is This?" (HB, LBW, MH, PH, TPH, UMH, WB)

THE NINTH LESSON

READING

From John 1:1–5: In the Beginning...

REFLECTION

(to be read by one voice)

> It is not over,
>   this birthing.
> There are always newer skies
>   into which
>   God can throw stars.
>
> When we begin to think
>   that we can predict the Advent of God,
>   that we can box the Christ
>   in a stable in Bethlehem,
>   that's just the time that God will be born
>   in a place we can't imagine and won't believe.
>
> Those who wait for God
>   watch with their hearts and not their eyes,
>   listening
>   always listening
>   for angel words.

> —Ann Weems,
> from *Kneeling in Bethlehem*[6]

CAROL

"It Came Upon a Midnight Clear"

SUGGESTED ALTERNATE HYMNS

"O Gladsome Light" (HB, LBW, PH, TPH, UMH, WB)

"O Word of God Incarnate" (HB, HUCC, LBW, MH, PH, TPH, UMH, WB)

BESTOWING THE BLESSING

NOTES

1. Opening words by Ted Loder from *Guerrillas of Grace*, © 1984 by LuraMedia, Inc., San Diego, CA 92121.

2. "The God Who Does Not Blame," reprinted from *Meditations with Julian of Norwich*, edited by Brendan Doyle, © 1983 by Bear & Co., Inc., P.O. Box 2860, Santa Fe, NM 87504.

3. "O Holy Spirit," reprinted from *Meditations with Hildegard of Bingen*, © 1982 by Bear & Co., Inc., P.O. Box 2860, Santa Fe, NM 87504.

4. "The Announcement" and Prayer Response are adapted from Miriam Therese Winter from *WomanWord: A Feminist Lectionary and Psalter*, © 1990 by Crossroad Publishing Co., 370 Lexington Ave., New York, NY 10017.

5. "Startled by a Holy Humming" by Carol Doran and Tom Troeger from *New Hymns for the Lectionary*, © 1987 by Oxford University Press, Inc.

6. "It Is Not Over . . ." by Ann Weems, from *Kneeling in Bethlehem*, © 1980 by Westminster Press.

2

WISE WOMEN BEARING PEACE

(Epiphany)

INTRODUCTION

The service that follows, held on the eve of war in the Persian Gulf, emerged as one of the most profoundly moving experiences we have ever shared as a community. In planning for an Epiphany celebration, we had begun to realize that the story of the Magis' journey in search of the newborn Christ, an inseparable part of the Christmas narrative, is nevertheless a patriarchal account reflective of its culture and time. How might the truth it contains be made accessible to women — and particularly to women long alienated from the institutional church and its traditional interpretation of the gospel, who flock hungrily to gatherings like Women, Word, and Song for spiritual nurture?

We began to muse about whether the journey of the Magi might have been different, and *how*, had it been a *women's* story. And so was born the idea of inviting the community to reframe the narrative, segment by segment, retaining the truth of it but retelling it as our own "new oral tradition." Just then, as so often (and so astonishingly) is the case, world events flared up to set a spark to faith history. In the days this service was taking shape, tensions escalated in the Persian Gulf. In the face of Saddam Hussein's defiance, the president of the United States declared an ultimatum, giving the Iraqi leader thirty-six hours beyond the time of our scheduled gathering to temper his position or to face bombing attacks from American forces.

Imminent war was deeply etched into the minds and consciences of the seventy-five peace-loving women who gathered under tiny "stars" strung across the ceiling of our darkened chapel on that chill January night. The ancient story we found ourselves telling for the first time was clearly apparent to all of us to be an inspiration of the Holy Spirit. Phrase by phrase (through a process delineated below, in the body of the service) the narrative was constructed . . . retold . . . further constructed . . . retold . . . until, when the final surprising sentence was spoken that plainly was the "Amen," we were struck silent — with tears on many faces — at the power of the gospel, which many of us could not have heard through Matthew's voice

31

alone. We share the story here, exactly as it came to be told that night, not as a model that must be slavishly copied (since *no* one can "choreograph" the voice of a community!) but as a testament to the enduring power of the Word to be heard even in the most fearful or oppressive social contexts.

> Long ago, women of wisdom from all over the earth began to gather together: mothers and grandmothers, sisters and daughters, cousins and aunts. They converged in order to witness and to midwife the birth of a holy little girl-child of mid-Eastern descent . . . perhaps an Iraqi.
>
> This was distressing to the Herods of the earth, who are *ever* distressed and fearful when women gather together: the male Herods because of their fear that someone might displace them, and the female Herods because someone *else* might be the fairest of them all. The Herods asked the wise women where this child was to be born: "Return and tell us," they said, "so that we may worship too!" (In other words, "Give *us* your wisdom.")
>
> The wise women went on and found the place and helped the birth to come about. And they brought with them gifts — corn, squash, beans, and bread — these symbolizing the interconnectedness of all of life, gifts that could be used to feed the whole world.
>
> So instead of the ancient gifts we've been told were brought — gold for royalty, frankincense for worship of divinity, and myrrh for the embalming of the dead — these women brought *other* gifts. Instead of royalty, they brought humility. Instead of worship, they brought partnership. Instead of death, they brought the knowledge of how to live.
>
> And when they had offered their gifts, knowing that they dare not go back to Herod and to the old ways, they made their home with this child . . . and thereby *came home* in a different way.

(*Here, we thought the story was over; until suddenly, from far back in the darkness, one woman's voice spoke the final, stunning words:*)

Because of that, there was no slaughter of the Innocents — and no Rachel weeping for her children.

PREPARATION

With the exception of this particular gathering, it has been our consistent discipline *not* to hold Women, Word, and Song services in a traditional worship space. We have found that there are many women who can no longer bring themselves to enter church sanctuaries, because of abusive experiences or oppressive memories connected with "church," but who, even yet, are women of deep faith, vital spirituality, and a longing for the Holy. While many other sisters would have no difficulty with traditional settings, it has been a serious concern for us that *all* of women's experience be respected — and that no obstacle be created to continue to bar "unchurched" women from their God. As we wrote in our first volume, "Worship in a feminist mode blesses and finds blessing in *unexpected* space such as parlor, lounge, or entryway; where the breaking open of old expectations and visual patterns allows for the in-breaking of the Spirit. . . . "

The decision to make an exception to our own practice in this instance was one with which we grappled for days. In the end, physical/structural needs of the service determined that it would be held in the church's chapel, where the glare of street lights would not intrude on the darkness we needed, and where the narrower width of the room would facilitate the stringing of tiny white Christmas tree lights from wall to wall across the ceiling.

To be most effective, then, the service should be planned for an area that can be darkened so that strings of white lights overhead (criss-crossed diagonally at random) may have a star-like effect. Overhead lights, if controlled by a rheostat, may be turned up after the service begins to a level just high enough for worshippers to read words of hymns; alternatively, it is possible to hold the gathering in darkness with select readers and/or solo voices (equipped with penlights) and singing parts. Capacity to play a cassette tape is needed. While the original service was conducted with worshippers seated in short rows of fixed pews, a more flexible, circular mode would be the preferable seating.

❧

MUSIC FOR REFLECTION

Cris Williamson, "One of the Light"[1]
Played on a cassette deck after worshippers are seated.

INVOCATION (unison)

> O God, the source of all insight,
> whose coming was revealed to the nations
> not among men of power
> but on a woman's lap;
> give us grace to seek you
> where you may be found,
> that the wisdom of this world may be humbled
> and discover your unexpected joy,
> through Jesus Christ. Amen.

> —Janet Morley,
> from *All Desires Known*[2]

INVITATION TO THE SEARCH

Epiphany is traditionally the time when the church celebrates the revealing of the Light. Joyce Rupp has taken the tradition of Epiphany and reflected upon it in a different way. Here are her words:

There is a story told in the Christian Scriptures of three astronomers who followed an immensely bright star (Matthew 2:1–12). They were so drawn by this star that they followed a hunch in their hearts that it would lead them to the Divine. So set were their hearts on this bright vision in the sky that they pursued it over great distances and through many struggles. Following the star meant that they had to do their traveling at night. They did not know where they would be led. They only knew that they had to follow. They lost sight of the star, and in great humility, they had to rely on other starseekers to tell them where to locate the star again.

This star "filled their hearts with delight" (Matthew 2:10). They continued to follow it in the darkness of the night, journeying until finally they found themselves at the feet of the one whom they had long sought. Surely Sophia must have danced a radiant star dance on that night when these weary travelers finally reached the goal of their long journey.

This story is so like my own inner one. I feel drawn to seek the Divine. I go mostly in the night, not being sure of the direction, or of what this God will look like, or where the journey will take me. I lose my way. Then I find others who have seen the star. They show me and guide me. I find the way again. And one day I discover God as the beloved, the one for whom I have so yearned. This may be the most unlikely of places, and perhaps just for a fleeting moment, but I know in the brief discovery that the journey has been worth it. My heart, like those seekers of long ago, is filled with delight. This discovery is usually a very brief experience. And so I continue on the journey of life with hope in my heart, seeking by the light of the star to have another glimpse of the beloved.

—Joyce Rupp, from *The Star in My Heart*[3]

SONG

O Day Full of Grace

O day full of grace, which we behold,
now gently to view as ascending;
thou over the earth thy reign unfold,
good cheer to all mortals lending,
That children of light in ev'ry clime
may prove that the night is ending.

How blest was that gracious midnight hour
when God in our flesh was given;

then flushed the dawn with light and pow'r
that spread o'er the darkened heaven;
Then rose o'er the earth that Sun divine
which gloom from our hearts hath driven.

Yea, were ev'ry tree endowed with speech,
and every leaflet singing,
they never with praise God's worth could reach,
though earth with their praise be ringing.
Who fully could praise "the Light of Life"
who light to our souls is bringing?

—words by Nicolai Gruntvig[4]

HEARING THE ANCIENT WORD: Matthew 2:1–12

Narrator: Now wise men from the East
came to Jerusalem to inquire:

Sage: Where is the newborn king of the Jews?
We have seen his star in the East
and we have come to worship him.

Narrator: When Herod the king
heard about this
he was deeply troubled,
as were many in Jerusalem
He called together the chief priests and scribes
and asked them,
"Where was the Christ to be born?"
And they answered,

Voice: "In Bethlehem of Judea.
So the prophet has spoken:
'You, Bethlehem,
in the land of Judah,
are no means least among
the leaders of Judah;
out of you will come a leader
who will govern Israel."

Narrator: Then Herod secretly summoned the sages,
seeking to know when the star had appeared.
And he sent them off to Bethlehem, saying:

Voice: "Search for the child,
and when you have found him,
come back and tell me where he is
so I too may worship him."

Narrator: They left the king and went their way,
              following the star they had seen in the East.
              They were filled with joy when the star stopped
              above the place where the child was living.
              They entered Mary's house
              and they saw the child with his mother,
              and they bowed down and worshipped him.
              They opened their treasures
              and offered to him gifts of gold
              and frankincense
              and myrrh.
              Then warned in a dream to avoid Herod,
              they returned to their home a different way.

                                                —Miriam Therese Winter,
                                                   from *WomanWord*

Response: O, Star of wonder, Star of night
              Star with royal beauty bright
              Westward leading, still proceeding
              Guide us to Thy perfect Light.

REINTERPRETING THE WORD

The leader invites the group to rethink the story as a woman-identified or woman-rooted one. She then "lines out" the narrative scene-by-scene (as indicated below), pausing after each segment to give worshippers adequate time to absorb the story line and then to voice a revised telling.

- Now wise men from the East came to Jerusalem to inquire: Where is the newborn king of the Jews? We have seen his star in the East and come to worship him.

- When Herod the king heard about this, he was deeply troubled as were many in Jerusalem. Why?

- Then Herod secretly summoned the wise men, seeking to know when the star had appeared. And he sent them off to Bethlehem saying, "Search for the child and when you have found him, come back and tell me where he is so I too may worship him."

- They opened their treasures and offered him gifts of gold (royalty) frankincense (worship) and myrrh (embalming for death).

- Then, warned in a dream to avoid Herod, they returned to their home by a different way.

A Wisdom Psalm

Leader: What good is the gold that gilds the affluent and undergirds a two-tier system in religion and in the world?

People: Follow the one who is simple and poor and politically unencumbered.

Leader: What good is the incense that burns with a flair on the altars of our own making?

People: Follow the one who worships Shaddai in spirit and in truth.

Leader: What good is the myrrh that masks the pain and embalms our dead intentions?

People: Follow the one who died and rose from the symbols of decay.

Leader: You will be offered sage advice about overpowering others.

People: Rather be overpowered by that power pressed to a cross.

Leader: The way that leads to the center of success is strewn with the slaughter of innocence.

People: The way home goes by a different path. Just follow the song of the star.

Leader: Wise are the ones who hear this word and do their best to keep it.

People: Wise are the daughters of wisdom, for they hold these things in their heart.

—Miriam Therese Winter,
from *WomanWord*[5]

Response (sung):

> O, Star of wonder, Star of night
> Star with royal beauty bright,
> Westward leading, still proceeding,
> Guide us to thy perfect Light.

THE OFFERING OF WISE WOMEN'S GIFTS

Here the leader reflects upon the identifying of the one great gift each of us knows in her heart that she has brought into the world in the year just past. The lighting of incense here provides sensory imagery, with the aroma filling the worship space.

When each has silently identified her gift, the community stands to face each other (rows facing alternately backward and forward if in fixed pews, so that pairs of women face each other across the back of a pew). Each woman names her gift to her partner, and the partner responds by placing hands on her shoulders and saying:

Holy are your gifts, my sister:
May the Star of wisdom guide you on.

SINGING

Blessing Song

May the blessing of God go before you.
May Her grace and peace abound.
May Her spirit live within you.
May Her love wrap you 'round.
May Her blessing remain with you always.
May you walk on holy ground.

—words and music by Miriam Therese Winter,
WomanPrayer/WomanSong[6]

CLOSING WORDS

A solo voice reads these words as a benediction.

A Psalm for the Lost and Found

Women, we have lost our God and now we go to find her. We will look among our relatives, our acquaintances, and we will search on our pilgrimage asking, "Where is our God?" We will retrace the routes of religion, and the known roads of our heritage. We will repeat the ancient prayers, asking "Where is our God?"

In the temples of tradition, in the midst of its interpreters, we will challenge and question their assumptions. We will show our strength as we reveal through personal testimony that in life's experience God is found, for She sojourns with us. When we find our God, we will worship. We have found her. She is with us. She is dwelling in our heart. Amen.

—Miriam Therese Winter,
adapted from *WomanWord*

❀

NOTES

1. "One of the Light," by Cris Williamson from the album *The Changer and the Changed,* © 1975 by Olivia Records, Box 12064, Oakland, CA 94604.

2. Invocation by Janet Morley from *All Desires Known,* © 1988 by Morehouse-Barlow, 78 Danbury Road, Wilton, CT 06897.

3. Reading from *The Star in My Heart* by Joyce Rupp. © 1990, LuraMedia, Inc., San Diego, CA 92121.

4. "O Day Full of Grace" is a song in the public domain. Music by C. E. F. Weyse, words by Nicolai Gruntvig. The authors found this piece in *Borning Cry:*

Psalms, Hymns, and Celebrations, vol. 1, by Ylvisaker, Inc., Box 321, Waverly, IA 50677.

5. Reading of Matthew 1:1–12 (adapted), "Wisdom Psalm" and "Psalm for the Lost and Found" are by Miriam Therese Winter from *Woman Word: A Feminist Lectionary and Psalter,* © 1990 by Crossroad Publishing Co., 370 Lexington Ave., New York, NY 10017.

6. "Blessing Song," words and music by Miriam Therese Winter from *WomanPrayer/WomanSong,* © 1987 by Crossroad Publishing Co., 370 Lexington Ave., New York, NY 10017.

SUGGESTED ALTERNATE HYMNS

"All My Heart This Night Rejoices" (HB, HUCC, LBW, MH, PH, TPH, WB)

"Bring We the Frankincense of Our Love" (TPH)

"Christ, Whose Glory Fills the Skies" (HB, LBW, MH, PH, TPH, UMH, WB)

"De Tierra Lejana Venimos" ("From a Distant Home") (TPH, UMH)

"Wellspring of Wisdom" (UMH)

"On This Day Earth Shall Ring" (HUCC, PH, TPH, UMH, WB)

"We Would See Jesus" (MH, PH, UMH)

"What Star Is This, with Beams So Bright?" (HUCC, PH, TPH, WB)

3

INHERITING THE PROMISE: THE DAUGHTERS OF ZELOPHEHAD

(Lent)

INTRODUCTION

"Now Zelophehad the son of Hepher had no sons, but daughters: and the names of the daughters of Zelophehad were Mahlah, Noah, Hoglah, Milcah, and Tirzah" (Num. 26:33). Extraordinary women they must have been, to have the courage to approach Moses to claim the inheritance that should be theirs — not by the provisions of law, but by the principles of justice! Extraordinary, too, for having their names recorded when so many biblical women have gone nameless. Had they had brothers, had Zelophehad received sons, they too would have passed away unknown to us.

Aside from their courageous alliance, however, little is known about them individually. What, other than blood ties, bound these women into the kind of partnership that could prevail against tradition? With their names alone as clues, worshippers are challenged in this service to use both biblical skills and imaginations to search for insight that can also empower us to stand together for what is right. The solidarity of sisters seems energized, rather than crippled, by an apparently wide diversity among the five as suggested by their names — the only clues left to us as to their identities.

The sisters seem to have been named after Canaanite cities, which, in turn, were often named after gods or goddesses. From the little that can be determined about the origin or meaning of their names, a sketchy picture begins to emerge for worshippers to carry forward in creative conversation as we celebrate their legacy together:

Tirzah: The name of the capital of the northern kingdom. The beauty of
    Tirzah is said to be "as comely as Jerusalem" (Song of Solomon 6:4).

Mahlah: "Weak one."

Milcah: "Queen, princess"; a title of the Babylonian goddess Ishtar.

Noah: "Out of the ground which Yahweh has cursed, this one shall bring us relief from our work and the toil of our hands." (Gen. 5:29)

Hoglah: "Partridge."

PREPARATION

Five blank "shields" (approximately 2' x 3' in dimension) must be prepared in advance from poster board, one to represent each daughter of Zelophehad. This service was prepared specifically for a conference on women in ministry, with almost one hundred participants in worship. While it requires significant preparation for both large and small groups, it is equally effective regardless of size. The dynamics of the subgroups will obviously vary, depending whether eight or twenty women are creating a shield together.

Since the Scriptures used in the service are not well known, it is helpful to have the passages printed on the front and back covers of the order of worship. Each worship bulletin must be numbered 1 through 5 to facilitate dividing into small groups during the service. A set of colored markers of various shades is required for each of the five groupings.

THE PROMISE OF GOD IN THE WILDERNESS

READING: Exodus 3:7–8

UNISON PRAYER

Promise us,
O God of the Exodus,
promise You will keep
Your promise,
for the land we seek
seems far from us
and the road we travel
is long.

Silence

Promise we will come
to the promised land
while we can still remember

the vision and the traditions
to which we once belonged.
Amen.

—Miriam Therese Winter,
Woman Wisdom

THE CENSUS

READING: Numbers 26:28-34, 52-55

(A census is taken to ascertain the strength of the tribes and to allot the land that is promised)

Voice 1: The sons of Joseph by their clans: Manasseh and Ephraim.

Voice 2: The descendants of Manasseh: of Machir, the clan of Machirites; and Machir was the Father of Gilead.

Voice 3: Of Gilead, the clan of the Gileadites. These are the descendants of Gilead:

Voice 4: Of Iezer, the clan of the Iezerites;

Voice 1: of Helek, the clan of the Helekites;

Voice 2: and of Asriel, the clan of the Asrielites;

Voice 3: and of Shechem, the clan of the Shechemites;

Voice 4: and of Shemida, the clan of the Shemidaites;

Voice 1: and of Hepher, the clan of the Hepherites.

Voice 3: Now Zelophehad son of Hepher had no sons, but daughters;

Voice 2: and the names of the daughters of Zelophehad were:

Voice 1: Mahlah,

Voice 2: Noah,

Voice 3: Hoglah,

Voice 4: Milcah,

Voice 2: and Tirzah.

All: These are the clans of Manasseh; the number of those enrolled was fifty-two thousand seven hundred.

Voice 1: The Lord spoke to Moses, saying: To these the land shall be apportioned for inheritance according to the number of names.

Voice 3: To a large tribe you shall give a large inheritance,

Voice 4:   and to a small tribe you shall give a small inheritance;

Voices 3 and 4:   Every tribe shall be given its inheritance according to its enrollment.

All: But the land shall be apportioned by lot; according to the names of their ancestral tribes they shall inherit.

HYMN

"Guide me, O Thou Great Jehovah," *The Presbyterian Hymnal*

A PSALM ABOUT THE PROMISED LAND

Group 1:   Lead me into the promised land.
I am sick unto death of bondage,
burdened by doubt and debt
and all those things
by which we are bound.

Group 2:   Give me a taste of milk and honey
in a cup running over.
It is time to replace the salted tears
that season my daily bread.

Group 1:   Lift up Your hand, O Mover of Mountains.
You can divide the waters
to let a whole new generation
pass over from slavery.

Group 2:   My heart is ready, O God,
my heart is ready with song and laughter,
ready to lead the victory dance
on the safe side of the sea.

Group 1:   Narrow the stream that divides what is
from the blessings that have been promised.

Group 2:   Shallow the rivulet separating us
from all that we might be.

Group 1:   On that day the lion and lamb
will be at peace within us.

Group 2:   On that day all good people
will climb the mountain of God.

Group 1:   Every home will have security,
every heart will have an advantage,

Group 2:   And no one will want for anything
in the household of God.

Group 1:   We will sing and bring to birth in each other
           the fruits of the new creation.

Group 2:   We will sow the seeds of Shalom
           among all the survivors of rape and war.

Group 1:   Praise be to You, Shekinah-Shaddai,
           for you are the Source of the promise

Group 2:   In You we come home to freedom.
           You are the Promised Land.

—Miriam Therese Winter,
Woman Wisdom[1]

THE INHERITANCE
AND THE DAUGHTERS' ACTION

READING

Numbers 26:33; 27:1-4

CREATION OF SYMBOLS OF EACH DAUGHTER

Worshippers are divided into groups each named for a different daughter. The discussion takes the shape of imaginative brainstorming on who the daughters were. (For example: I am TIRZAH, meaning "the beautiful one." My sisters see me as.... But I see myself as....) Designations for the other four discussions groups are as follows:

- I am MAHLAH meaning "the weak one"
- I am MILCAH meaning "the royal one"
- I am NOAH meaning "the one who helps"
- I am HOGLAH meaning "the free spirit"

Following discussion, each group creates a crest symbolizing the particular woman. In designing, participants are asked to consider what words or phrases (from their brainstorming) best describe the woman. What color might symbolize her? Is there a particular animal or plant that comes to mind? What other symbols are appropriate to her qualities?

After each group completes the shield of symbols the following passage from Numbers is read.

THE RESPONSE OF GOD: Numbers 27:5-8

Moses brought their case before the Lord. And the Lord said to Moses, "The daughters of Zelophehad are right; you shall give them possession of an inheritance among their father's brethren and cause the inheritance of their father to pass to them. And you shall say to the people of Israel, 'If a man dies, and has no son, then you shall cause his inheritance to pass to his daughter.'"

SONG

"Standing Before Us," Carole Etzler[2]

The worship leader calls upon each daughter. A representative of each group describes her group's shield. As each is presented the worship leader takes notes on what is described. These will be used later to formulate a "commission" for each group. Between each presentation a verse and chorus of "Standing Before Us" is sung.

1. The Voice of Tirzah

These are the women who throughout the decades
have led us and helped us to know —
Where we have come from and where we are going,
the women who've helped us to grow.

> CHORUS:
> Standing before us, Making us strong.
> Lending their wisdom to help us along,
> Sharing a vision. Sharing a dream,
> Touching our thoughts, touching our lives,
> like a deep flowing stream.

2. The Voice of Mahlah

These are the women who joined in the struggle,
Angry and gentle and wise.
These are the women who called us to action,
Who called us to open our eyes.

> CHORUS

3. The Voice of Milcah

These are the women who nurtured our spirits,
The ones on whom we could depend.
These are the women who gave us their courage,
Our mentors, our sisters, our friends.

> CHORUS

4. The Voice of Noah

These are a few of the women who led us.
We know there have been many more.

We name but a few, yet we honor them all,
Those women who went on before.

> CHORUS

5. *The Voice of Hoglah*

> CHORUS

PRAYER OF EMPOWERMENT (unison)

> Empower me
> to be a bold participant,
> rather than a timid saint in waiting,
> in the difficult ordinariness of now;
> to exercise the authority of honesty,
> rather than to defer to power,
> or deceive to get it;
> to influence someone for justice,
> rather than impress anyone for gain;
> and, by grace, to find treasures
> of joy, of friendship, of peace
> hidden in the fields of the daily
> you give me to plow.

> —Ted Loder,
> from *Wrestling the Light*[3]

THE COMMISSIONING OF THE DAUGHTERS

At this point the worship leader asks each daughter/group to rise. Then, using the notes taken earlier, each daughter/group is commissioned. Each commission ends with the unison response:

> May Your Strength Liberate Us All.

SONG

"Guide My Feet," *The Presbyterian Hymnal*

BLESSING

Remember Sisters: Within the land of Israel daughters will always be permitted to inherit the land of their fathers because the daughters of Zelophehad dared to question the law as it was and sought to change it.

> —Alice Bach and J. Cheryle Exum,
> from *Miriam's Well*[4]

NOTES

1. Unison Prayer and "Psalm about the Promised Land" by Miriam Therese Winter, from *Woman Wisdom,* © 1991 by Crossroad Publishing Co., 370 Lexington Ave., New York, NY 10017.

2. "Standing Before Us," by Carole Etzler from the album *Thirteen Ships,* produced by Sisters Unlimited, Inc., P.O. Box 826, Springfield, VT 05156

3. Prayer of Empowerment by Ted Loder from *Wrestling the Light,* © 1991 LuraMedia Inc., San Diego, CA 92121. Used with permission of publisher.

4. The Blessing is from *Miriam's Well* by Alice Bach and J. Cheryle Exum, © 1991 Delacorte Press, 666 Fifth Ave., New York, NY 10103. Used by permission of publisher.

SUGGESTED ALTERNATE HYMNS

"God of Our Life" (HB, MH, PH, TPH, WB)

"Great God, We Sing That Mighty Hand" (HB, HUCC, PH, TPH)

"Lord, You Have Been Our Dwelling Place" (HB, TPH)

"Many Gifts, One Spirit" (UMH)

"O God, Our Faithful God" (LBW, TPH, WB)

"We Need Each Other's Voice To Sing" (NHLC)

4

PROCLA

(Lent)

PROCLA: DO NOT DENY THE TRUTH OF YOUR DREAMS
DO NOT DENY THE TRUTH OF YOURSELF

INTRODUCTION

Always, women were there. They were seldom named, or, if named, rarely described. But they were there . . . walking the same roads, attending to the teachings, watching at the cross. And there were individual women like Procla, the wife of Pilate, whose husband lives in infamy for having washed his hands of Jesus. It was Procla who attempted to stir him awake, to gird his will to resist crowd psychology: a woman who paid attention to her own dreams, her intuition for justice, the truth of her inner voice.

What if the will of Procla had prevailed? But Pilate washed his own hands of this dilemma — what to do with one whom he did not believe was guilty. Because no one else would enable him to let Jesus go, he absolved himself for not being able to do it alone. This service of worship remembers the woman who tried to intervene, by transforming Pilate's act of cowardice into a vehicle of grace: not to absolve, but to cleanse. Perhaps thereby the result can be different for all the innocent Christs in the world today.

PREPARATION

Participants are seated in semicircular rows facing a round center table. Three large basins rest on top of a plain white cloth covering the table, equidistant from one other, each two-thirds full of warm water scented with a few drops of bath oil. A dry hand towel is folded next to each basin.

The handwashing ritual in the service may be done in silence. However, if background music is to be used, leaders should determine whether a single *a capella* voice or a tape recording will provide it.

❀

48

GATHERING MUSIC

LIGHTING OF THE CHRIST CANDLE

GATHERING WORDS

Leader: O Lord, open my eyes.

People: So I might see the vision of your truth.

Leader: O Lord, open my ears.

People: And I will hear your word.

Leader: O Lord, open my lips.

People: And my mouth shall proclaim your truth.

SONG

"Once to Every Heart and Nation," words from *Inclusive Language Hymns*

THE STORY OF PROCLA

Matthew 27:15–26

READING

Dreams Denied

How did Pilate's wife
know about Jesus?
From rumors alone?
Or word from her maidservants?
Or some chance meeting
with this memorable man?
She said that she had suffered
much because of him —
all in a dream.
But was it a dream only?
Was her conscience hurt
because she lacked the courage
of Joanna
to leave her palace post
and follow the Crown Prince
of truth and liberation?
She was convinced
that he was innocent
of public crimes

but not unguilty
of stirring her heart to dreams
she had denied.

—Thomas John Carlisle,
from *Beginning with Mary*[1]

REFLECTION

Pilate asked "What is Truth?" (Gospel of John) and yet it was his wife who spoke the truth. The opposite of "Truth" (*alethē*) in Greek is "Forgetting" (*lethē*). Pilate's wife, Procla, knew the truth from her dreams, and she paid attention to them. Pilate washed his hands of all responsibility for Jesus. He "washed his hands" of the "truth" in the hope he could forget it.

He really knew the truth but could not admit it.

He hoped that the crowd would solve his "problem."

He hoped that Herod would solve his "problem."

He hoped that Jesus will solve the problem.

As the daughters of Procla we wash *our* hands so that we might be able to begin again.

What do we risk when we acknowledge the truth?

RITUAL OF HAND WASHING

Pilate's handwashing is "reframed" (literally turning the story around) into a ritual of washing each other's hands — to cleanse one another of complicity with all that kills Life in the world. Women approach the table and wash each other's hands in silence; when one has her hands washed, she turns and washes the hands of the next woman, and so on. The melody of "What Wondrous Love Is This?" may be played during the Handwashing.

UNISON PRAYER

God our Life-Giver
Again and again we find ourselves stuck
in old patterns of domination and submission;
we stay resenting our powerlessness
or guilt-ridden by our power.

Give us courage to believe that
change is possible:
let us so wash one another's hands as friends
that the fragrance of our ministry may
fill the whole church;
and free us with the symbol of slavery
to make a world where no one is in bondage.

In the name of the one who died to give us life,
Jesus Christ, Amen.

—Janet Morley,
"Celebrating Women" (adapted)[2]

MUSIC

"Sometimes I Wish," words and music by Carole Etzler[3]

CALL/RESPONSE

After each "Voice" reads a line, participants repeat it.

Voice 1: You are in our womb,

Voice 2: the Womb of Womanbody-Womansoul.

Voice 1: We call you forth into life

Voice 2: and greet you with a new name . . .

Voice 1: Majestic Stag drinking cool waters from River of Life,

Voice 2: be born and live!

Voice 1: Great Eagle poised upon the highest peaks of the Ever-lasting Mountain,

Voice 2: be born and soar!

Voice 1: Strong and brilliant Rock, survive!

Voice 2: Dreamer of new worlds, dream on!

Voice 1: Bringer of laughter, tears, and song,

Voice 2: we call you forth.

Voice 1: Woman of visions and of words,

Voice 2: we call you forth.

Voice 1: Man fathering hope in the souls of many,

Voice 2: we call you forth!

Voice 1: Whatever kind of death this birthing requires of you,

Voice 2: we offer you our energy,

Voice 1: our womanstrength,

Voice 2: and the secure space of this womanwomb

Voice 1: to give you courage and sustenance for the passage.

Voice 2: Remember us when you are born anew!

—Christin Lore Weber,
adapted from *Blessings:
A WomanChrist Reflection on the Beatitudes*[4]

SONG

"What Wondrous Love Is This?" *The Presbyterian Hymnal*

PSALM OF INTEGRITY

Unison: O God, be my integrity
in the midst of lies
and all the deceitful practices that abound.

Group 1: Shield me from the dishonesty
that permeates our culture
and pervades the halls of power.
Let me speak Your truth unflinchingly
aloud in public places.

Group 2: Let me call to accountability
all those who claim to keep Your word
yet violate our trust.
In the rites of life and religion,
may I never turn to other gods
or empty ritual making.

Group 3: In all my daily dealings,
may I never trade on pretense
or make outlandish claims,
or hide behind the flimsy veil of a false humility. May I
never deny Your grace in me
or credit other sources.

Unison: May I never forget that a lust for power
pinned You to a cross.
Deliver us all from a public ethic
divorced from private practice.
Lead us, O God, to confess our failings,
to seek and ask forgiveness,
and help us begin again.

—Miriam Therese Winter,
WomanWord[5]

CLOSING WORDS

We do not know what it took, how much agony, how many years, for Procla to find peace at last after the death of "that righteous man." Let us remember her as we sing our prayer, that with clean hands we may tenderly heal the world and so find a peace beyond our understanding.

CLOSING SONG

"Dona Nobis Pacem" (sung as a round)

❀

NOTES

1. "Dreams Denied," by Thomas John Carlisle from *Beginning with Mary,* © 1986 William B. Eerdmans Publishing Co., 255 Jefferson Ave., S.E., Grand Rapids, MI 49503. Used with permission of publisher.

2. Unison Prayer by Janet Morley from "Celebrating Women," published by Women in Theology and Movement for the Ordination of Women, Holy Trinity House, Orsett Terrace, London W2 6AH, England. © 1986. Used by permission of author.

3. "Sometimes I Wish," words and music by Carole Etzler. © 1974, as sung by Jim and Jean Strathdee on the album *In Loving Partnership,* produced by Caliche Records, P.O. Box 1735 Ridgecrest, CA 93555.

4. The Call/Response is adapted from a prayer found in *Blessings: A Woman-Christ Reflection on the Beatitudes,* by Christin Lore Weber, © 1989 by Christin Lore Weber. Reprinted by permission of HarperCollins Publishers, Inc.

5. "Psalm of Integrity" by Miriam Therese Winter, adapted from *Woman-Word: A Feminist Lectionary and Psalter,* © 1990 by Crossroad Publishing Co., 370 Lexington Ave., New York, NY 10017.

SUGGESTED ALTERNATE HYMNS

"Ah, Holy Jesus" (HB, HUCC, LBW, MH, PH, TPH, UMH, WB)

"Go to Dark Gethsemane" (HB, HUCC, LBW, MH, PH, TPH, UMH)

"Let There Be Light" (HB, HUCC, LBW, PH)

"My Song Is Love Unknown" (HUCC, LBW, PH, TPH)

"O Sacred Head, Now Wounded" (HB, HUCC, vs. 1–3; LBW, vs. 1–3; MH, PH, TPH, UMH, WB)

5

THE TOUCH OF CHRIST

(Eastertide)

INTRODUCTION

Time and again throughout the accounts of his ministry, Jesus was approached by people suffering from all sorts of infirmities and diseases. When he touched them, they were made whole, often rendered "clean" — and therefore once again acceptable as members of the worshipping community. In many cases, because he had *touched*, Jesus himself became unclean. Yet this fact is never mentioned in the narrative; Jesus is never quoted as being concerned about ritual "uncleanness."

The membrane-thin protective gloves worn by each worshipper in this service are symbolic reminders of the ever-so-slight barrier between each of us and other persons. In life we wear protection — sometimes literally, but more often figuratively. Not quite touching, not quite risking, we take precautions without consciously considering what or whom we are protecting.

In dialogue with contemporary life, the metaphor takes on extra power and poignancy for women who wear such gloves in their daily work of feeding, nursing, or caring for others — as well as for those who have watched a loved one suffer from AIDS or HIV-related illness, touched only by caregivers with carefully gloved hands.

The worship experience that follows allows us to feel with our bare hand the implications of a guarded spirit. And it asks us what it might mean to "remove the glove" *ourselves* and risk a newly vulnerable way of being in the world without a self-defensive layer around our hearts.

PREPARATION

The worship space is arranged in a large circle. In the center, a round table holds four large basins of warm water, two small bowls of scented oil, folded hand towels, candles.

As worshippers gather, each is given one surgical-type glove to wear on her right hand. When the service opens, worshippers are asked to hold hands around the circle so that each woman's gloved right hand is grasping another's, and her bare left hand is held by her neighbor's gloved hand.

❁

GATHERING MUSIC

Worship begins with the hearing of "Psalm 23" sung by Bobby McFerrin on the album *Medicine Man*.[1]

GOD'S CREATIVE HAND

Leader: In the beginning, God made the world:

Voice 1: made it and mothered it,

Voice 2: shaped it and fathered it;

Voice 3: filled it with seed and with signs of fertility,

Voice 4: filled it with love and its folk with ability.

Voice 1: All that is green, blue, deep and growing,

All: God's is the hand that created you.

Voice 2: All that is tender, firm, fragrant, and curious,

All: God's is the hand that created you.

Voice 3: All that crawls, flies, swims, walks or is motionless,

All: God's is the hand that created you.

Voice 4: All that speaks, sings, cries, laughs or keeps silence,

All: God's is the hand that created you.

Leader: All that suffers, lacks, limps or longs for an end.

All: God's is the hand that created you.

Leader: The world belongs to God;

All: the earth and its people belong to God.

—from *The Iona Community Worship Book*[2]

SONG

"Creating God Your Fingers Trace," *The Presbyterian Hymnal*

UNISON PRAYER

In the beginning was God,
In the beginning
the source of all that is
In the beginning
God yearning

God moaning
God laboring
God giving birth
God rejoicing
And God loved what she had made
And God said,
    "It is good."
And God, knowing that all that is good is shared
held the earth tenderly in her arms
God yearned for relationship.
God longed to share the good earth.
And humanity was born in the yearning of God.
We were born to share the earth.

—Carter Heyward,
Our Passion for Justice[3]

ANCIENT ONES FORMED BY THE HAND OF GOD

Voice 1:   "When Jesus came down from the mountain, great crowds followed him; and behold a leper came to him and knelt before him, saying, "Lord, if you will, you can make me clean." (Matt. 8:1–2)

Voice 2:   "And they brought to Jesus a man who was deaf and had an impediment in his speech; and they besought him to lay his hand upon him." (Mark 7:32)

Voice 3:   "And there was a woman who had a spirit of infirmity for eighteen years; she was bent over and could not fully straighten herself. And when Jesus saw her, he called her. . . ." (Luke 13:11)

Voice 4:   "And they came to Bethsaida. And some people brought to Jesus a blind man, and begged him to touch him. (Mark 8:22)

OUR RESPONSE TO THOSE UNLIKE US
CREATED BY THE HAND OF GOD

The worship leader invites participants to form small groups or to discuss with the person next to them the following question:

Hearing this much of each story, how do you understand God as our creator?

TOUCHED BY THE HAND OF CHRIST

Voice 1:   And Jesus stretched out his hand and touched me, saying, "I will; be clean." And immediately my leprosy was cleansed.

Voice 2:   Jesus took me aside and put his fingers in my ears, and spat and touched my tongue. Then Jesus looked up to heaven, sighed, and I heard him say: "Ephphatha," which means "be opened." My ears were opened and my tongue was released, and I could speak for the very first time.

Voice 3:   Jesus placed his hands on me and immediately I could stand up straight. I laughed and cried at the same time, praising God.

Voice 4:   Jesus took me by the hand and led me out of the village. Then . . . he placed his hands on my eyes. I strained my eyes and I realized I could see. I saw everything clearly.

TO USE OUR HANDS TO TOUCH

We each wear a protective glove such as worn by food handlers. It is a glove that protects the person being served, as well as the server. In life we wear "protective gloves": the ever-so-slight barrier between each of us and another person. Not quite touching. . . . Not quite risking. . . . Taking precautions. Who are we in need of protecting? What are we protecting?

In each case Jesus does touch the person and they are healed, made whole, able to be a part of the worshipping community again. But in each case, by touching Jesus becomes unclean.

What does it mean to remove the glove? What are the protective layers that keep us from touching another in need, to be vulnerable, to remove the protective layer?

SONG

"Here I Am," *The Presbyterian Hymnal*
As worshippers sing this hymn they are invited to remove their gloves.

ANOINTING OUR HANDS FOR MINISTRY

When the hymn is completed, the invitation is given to come to the table in pairs (four pairs at a time), wash and dry each other's hands, and then anoint them with oil using the following Affirmation:

Anoint our hands to hold and heal the many lives that are broken to bring hope into hopelessness.

BLESSING

❈

NOTES

1. "Psalm 23" by Bobby McFerrin, from the album "Medicine Man," Capitol Records, Inc. © 1990.

2. The opening litany is from *The Iona Community Worshipbook,* © 1988 by Iona Community/Wild Goose Publications, Pearce Institute, 840 Govan Road, Glasgow G51 3UT, Scotland.

3. Excerpt from *Our Passion for Justice,* by Carter Heyward, © 1984 by Pilgrim Press, 700 Prospect Ave. E., Cleveland, OH 44115.

SUGGESTED ALTERNATE HYMNS

"All Things Bright and Beautiful" (HB, MH, PH, TPH, UMH)

"God of the Sparrow" (TPH, UMH)

"God Who Stretched the Spangled Heavens" (TPH, UMH, vs. 1, 3, 4)

"How Firm a Foundation" (HB, HUCC, LBW, MH, PH, TPH, UMH, WB)

"Joyful, Joyful, We Adore Thee" (HB, HUCC, LBW, MH, PH, TPH, UMH, WB)

"Many and Great, O God" (MH, TPH, UMH)

6

THE RECLAIMING OF MARTHA

(Eastertide)

INTRODUCTION

In John 11:1–45 Jesus responds to Martha's stubborn, passionate faith that he is no ordinary person with this revelation of himself, "I am the resurrection and the life . . . ," and Martha responds with a confession of Christ that stands out as a special climax in the New Testament: "You are the Christ, the Son of God, who has come into the world."

Thus John placed the confession of Christ on the lips of a woman, a woman who was known for her openness, her strength, and her practical nature. This confession is found in only one other place in the gospels, where it is spoken by Peter. Martha was a tenacious, wise, combative, competent, emancipated woman with many practical responsibilities in the community.

In remembering this story John throws overboard our traditional image of Martha: he restores to life the aggressive, disturbing, sage, active Martha, who went against all conventions: mistress of the house, housewife, apostle, the woman who stands beside Peter in her own right.

In the Middle Ages she was often painted as the proud housewife, with a fettered dragon stretched out at her feet.

The legend is that Martha eventually found her way to southern France, where she lived an ascetic life in charge of a convent. She preached, healed the sick, and raised a dead person who had drowned attempting to swim a river to hear her preach.

There is an ancient legend that Martha overcame a dragon who was the embodiment of evil, the demonic, the old order. The inhabitants of the countryside asked her to kill a man-eating dragon called Tarascus, "half animal and half fish," fatter than an ox and longer than a horse, with teeth like swords, that lay submerged in the Rhone and killed anyone who tried to cross. St. Martha went out against the dragon, sprinkled him with holy water, and set a cross before him, whereupon he was conquered and stood like a tame lamb. Martha bound him with her girdle. Martha does not trample or kill the dragon, but binds it. Martha marks the symbolic beginning of another way of dealing with evil: not its annihilation but its redemption, the transformation of the underside."

—Adapted from Elisabeth Moltmann-Wendel, *The Women around Jesus*[1]

The emphasis of this worship gathering is upon Mary and Martha as true partners. Although the sisters each played a significant role in biblical and church history, too often the community of faith has dismissed Martha, trivializing her as nagging and unspiritual because of the "women's work" in which she was engaged on one particular day. With this portrayal, the church has inadvertently dismissed (and demeaned) many, many women who identify with the practical ministries of daily life. This service is meant to affirm *every* woman's spiritual role and to encourage women of all vocations to think and write theologically.

PREPARATION

For this service each person will need a copy of the chart from *Creating Fresh Images for Preaching* by Tom Troeger (see below p. 63, two 5" x 8" index cards, and a pen. The excerpt above from *The Women around Jesus* could be printed in the bulletin. For many women this is new information, so it is helpful to have it in writing. It will be important to elicit from the participants what they recall of the Mary/Martha story and then to contrast that with the biblical evidence. (Mary Cartledge-Hayes in her book *To Love Delilah,* for example, contrasts our conventional wisdom with the biblical evidence in a very effective way.) The readings need not be printed but may be read by the worship leader during the service.

❃

GATHERING WORDS

O God,
you call us to commitment
even at the point of despair.
Give us the faith of Martha
to find in our anger and loss
a truthful place to proclaim you,
our resurrection and life
through Jesus Christ. Amen.

—Janet Morley,
All Desires Known[2]

UNISON PRAYER

O Sensitive Spirit,
Sister Spirit,
You inhabit my soul

and the soul of my sisters.
Be the bond that binds us together
through the tough times
of our liberation.
Be the Spirit of solidarity
at the heart of our global spirit.
Make us one
in one another
through the unity of Your presence
in all the varied prayers and practices
of our graced diversity.
Fill us, fulfill us,
and free us
from all that hurts or hinders
Your free-flowing force within us.
Come, Sister Spirit,
be with us all
now and forever.
Amen.

—Miriam Therese Winter,
WomanWord[3]

THE CONVENTIONAL WISDOM: MARY VS. MARTHA

*The leader invites participants to tell their versions of the Mary and Martha story.
What do they recall? What feelings do they have as they remember the story?*

SCRIPTURE

John 11:1–6, 17–44

READING

I Am Woman – Hear Me

I can simultaneously
smile at my sister
check a child's head
for fever
ascertain that the bread
is not burning
urge the cat from the door
with the toe of my sandal
note that the hem
of my robe is torn
and talk to you

of things visible,
invisible, and
as yet undreamed.
I may seem scattered
but if you should call
when my sister is not here
when the child is not here
when the bread is not baking
and the cat not at the door
then I will sit down
and talk to you
of things visible,
invisible, and
as yet undreamed.

—Mary Cartledge-Hayes,
from *To Love Delilah*[4]

THE WISDOM OF PARTNERSHIP VS. COMPETITION

This exercise is done twice. First it is experienced with minimal explanation, merely as part of worship. Then the group is led through the guided meditation and invited to write again. Both the content and the process allow for wonderful reflection and discussion.

The purpose of this exercise is to help participants to focus their hearts, minds, and spirits so that they will be enabled to write a prayer. The speaker must speak in a slow soft voice. The chart below (p. 63) is distributed to each person before beginning the guided imagery.

MEDITATIONS AND PRAYERS: Text for leader's use

Please allow yourself to come to a calm, quiet space inside yourself. Let the concerns of the day subside for now. As you are relaxing, I would like to guide you with some imagery.

Imagine you and me sitting quietly by a still pond deep in a forest on a clear, comfortable day. We've been sitting for a long time, silently, without needing to speak. Just being quiet, feeling the air, soft and pleasant against the skin, with the smells of the forest around us. The forest is very still, except for the sounds of an occasional bird and only the slightest movement of the air. The face of the pond is still; the surface, mirrorlike. In that mirror we can see still clouds. Shifting focus, we can look through the mirror, seeing the pebbles at the bottom of the pond. As we're sitting, not speaking, you notice a leaf that's being carried by the wind from high in a tree. It's turning slowly, falling gently from the clouds toward the pond. In the pond, another leaf, a mirror leaf, is rising slowly from the bottom, moving toward the surface. The two leaves move together, meeting exactly where the water meets the air. They come gently together and at the spot, a small wave ripples out and moves toward the edges of the pond. There, in the shallow water at the edges, the wave embraces the grass, which dances its delight. You notice now that it is God who is next to you. And as you sit there together, God speaks to you and says: "You and I are partners. We are partners in creation."[5]

This last statement can be repeated after about twenty seconds. Participants are then led through this exercise in creating a prayer:

DIRECTIONS FOR USING THIS CHART

Pick one word in each column to form a prayer that represents your dominant relationships with God. If you cannot find the precise word you want in a column, supply your own. But limit it to one word, no long phrases or hyphenated constructions. The struggle to find a single word will force greater clarity within you.

—Thomas Troeger[6]

Image of God

			Image of Self	
Eternal	God	(your)	believing	daughter
Loving	Lord		doubting	son
Judging	Christ		angry	child
Tender	Jesus		happy	disciple
Demanding	Spirit		seeking	friend
Healing	Love		trusting	priest
Heavenly	Being		hurting	creature
Earthly	Mother		thankful	servant
Unknown	Father		anxious	follower
Intimate	Savior		peaceful	rebel

Image of Communication

prays for	love
cries for	faith
demands	money
wants	food
needs	meaning
despairs of	comfort
wishes for	understanding
doubts	forgiveness
wonders about	joy
thanks you for	health

After participants have had time to write their prayers, gently invite them to share their writings.

CLOSING PRAYER

The Middle Time

Between the exhilaration of Beginning . . .
And the satisfaction of Concluding,
Is the Middle-Time
of Enduring . . . Changing . . . Trying . . .
Despairing . . . Continuing . . . Becoming.

Jesus Christ was the One of God's Middle-Time.
Between Creation and . . . Accomplishment.
Through him God said of Creation,
"Without mistake."
And of Accomplishment,
"Without doubt."

And we in our Middle-Times of Wondering and Waiting,
Hurrying and Hesitating, Regretting and Revising,
We who have begun many things . . . and seen but few completed,
We who are becoming more . . . and less —
Through the evidence of God's Middle-Time
Have a stabilizing hint
That we are not mistakes,
That we are irreplaceable,
That our Being is of interest,
And our Doing is of purpose,
That our Being and our Doing
are surrounded by Amen.
Jesus Christ is the Completer
of unfinished people
with unfinished work
in unfinished times.

May he keep us from us from sinking, from ceasing,
from wasting, from solidifying,
That we may be for him
Experimenters, Enablers, Encouragers,
And Associates in Accomplishment.

—Lona Fowler,
Images: Women in Transition[7]

NOTES

1. Excerpt adapted from *The Women around Jesus* by Elisabeth Moltmann-Wendel, © 1982 by Crossroad Publishing Co., 370 Lexington Ave., New York, NY 10017.

2. Gathering words by Janet Morley from *All Desires Known*, © 1988 by Morehouse-Barlow, 78 Danbury Road, Wilton, CT 06897.

3. Unison Prayer by Miriam Therese Winter from *WomanWord: A Feminist Lectionary and Psalter*, © 1990 by Crossroad Publishing Co., 370 Lexington Ave., New York, NY 10017.

4. "I Am Woman – Hear Me," by Mary Cartledge-Hayes from *To Love Delilah*, © 1990 by LuraMedia, Inc., San Diego, CA 92121. Used with permission of publisher.

5. The guided imagery exercise is by Ron Kuretz, originator of Hokomi Therapy and author of the book by the same title. Hakomi of Ashland, P.O. Box 537, Ashland, OR 97520. The authors discovered this exercise in *The Partnership Way* by Riane Eisler and David Loye. This is a practical companion for *The Chalice and the Blade*.

6. The chart used for writing prayers is from *Creating Fresh Images for Preaching* by Thomas H. Troeger, © 1982 by Judson Press, Valley Forge, PA 19481. Used by permission of Judson Press.

7. "The Middle Time," by Lona Fowler from *Images: Women in Transition*, edited by Janis Grana, © 1976 by The Upper Room, 1908 Grand Ave., Nashville, TN 37203

SUGGESTED ALTERNATE HYMNS

"Be Thou My Vision" (HB, PH, TPH, WB, UMH)

"Help Us Accept Each Other" (TPH, UMH)

"Here I Am, Lord" (TPH, UMH)

"How Clear Is Our Vocation, Lord" (TPH)

"O Jesus, I Have Promised" (HB, LBW, MH, PH, TPH, UMH)

"Woman in the Night" (UMH)

"We Need Each Other's Voice to Sing" (NHLC)

7

"CATCH THE WIND"

(Pentecost)

INTRODUCTION

The available imagery and resources for services at Pentecost provide a rich repository from which to draw. The coming of the Holy Spirit in the lives of believers as wind, flame, stillness, and water of life could yield endless ideas for the expression of joyful praise to this God who reaches toward us by every sensuous means. (We use the term "sensuous" here in its original sense, originated by the poet John Milton and elaborated upon by Dr. Virginia Mollenkott in her book *Sensuous Spirituality: Out from Fundamentalism:*

> In his tract *Of Reformation* (1641), Milton spoke of the body as the sensuous colleague of the soul; and in his pamphlet *Of Education* (1644), he described excellent poetry as "simple, sensuous, and passionate" (*Oxford English Dictionary*)....I use the word *sensuous* in both of these senses: to mean *embodied* or *physical,* as in the first usage; but also to mean linguistically concrete, direct, appealing to the senses, and concerned with beauty and justice, as in the second....The pleasure-hatred and erotophobia of most Western religion is unjust to the body itself, devaluing the means by which the spirit makes its impact in the world. (22)

Beginning with the primary image of the Spirit of God as *ruach* — breath, wind — this service began to unfold. When we pondered how to bring *wind* inside a room and make it felt on the skin and visible in the air, the vehicle that suggested itself was a kite. Fluttering in the breezes created by oscillating fans, kites became stunning images of our lives touched by a Spirit that blows where She will, as we strive for lives oriented in such a way that they too will "catch the Wind."

PREPARATION

For this service, the worship bulletin itself becomes a part of the creative process. It is printed on 8½" x 14" sheets, with the front page blank. On the back of the front page is printed the song "Spirit"; and over the music are superimposed dotted "fold" lines that will enable the worshipper to fold it into the shape of a kite. (Later in the service, the kite is embellished with the words of the *cinquain* poetry to be written by the individual worshipper.)

The worship area is set up in circular form, with a number of large oscillating fans set around the room — some on stands and others at floor level. Five large, colorful kites are randomly suspended from the ceiling with clear fishing line, positioned in relation to the moving fans so that long kite tails (which may be augmented with crepe paper streamers) will flutter and stream as the breeze moves across the space.

A round table in the center of the circle holds three red pillar candles, unlit, at varying heights; and a "skirt" of crepe paper streamers is taped around the table edge so that the red/orange streamers also ripple in the breeze. A supply of pencils or markers and clear tape should be available.

Lilting, meditative music plays as worshippers enter. The following words are printed at the beginning of the order of worship:

> Jesus said, "The wind blows where it chooses, and you hear the sound of it, but you do not know where it comes from or where it goes. So it is with everyone who is born of the Spirit." (John 3:8)

❁

LIGHTING OF CANDLES

Three women come forward to the table, and each in turn reads a portion of the litany and lights one of the three candles.

First: I will light a light
in the name of God
who lit the world
and breathed the breath of life into me.

All: In the God
who lit the world.

Second: I will light a light
in the name of the Christ
who saved the world
and stretched out a hand to me.

All: In the Christ
who saved the world.

Third: I will light a light
in the name of the Spirit
who encompasses the world
and blesses my soul with yearning.

All: In the Spirit
              who encompasses the world.

Three voices: We will light three lights
                  for the trinity of love:

All: God above us,
              God beside us,
              God beneath us:
              The beginning,
              the end,
              the everlasting one.
              blessed be Her name! Amen.

                                              —Adapted from
                                   Iona Community Worshipbook[1]

INVOKING THE SPIRIT

The leader offers a guided meditation, ending each segment with a short sentence prayer. The prayers need not be printed in the order of worship unless the community is asked to read them in unison.

Meditation: With your inner eye, envision the person or community who most bring joy to you by their presence in your life.

Prayer: Spirit of joy, through you Christ lives in us, and we in Christ.

Meditation: Now picture one person who has taught you most about the power of love, and sense the fullness of your gratitude to her/him.

Prayer: Spirit of love, you bind us in love to Yourself and to those around us. In marriage and partnership, in family and friendship we live out Your love.

Meditation: Allow all your senses to be open to the presence of the community surrounding you — seen and unseen, those living and those who have gone on ahead of us.

Prayer: Spirit of the body of Christ, you unite us into a community of faith through Your lifegiving grace and hope.

Meditation: Now, in silence, imagine and invoke the disparate peoples of the earth, especially those who struggle against oppression and want — eastern Europeans, Africans, tribal peoples of the far North and the Pacific, Latin Americans, Asians — and be aware of them as being your own flesh and blood.

Prayer: Spirit in the world, You comfort us and draw us into closer relationship with one another.

Meditation: Finally, focus your mind's eye on a candle flame. See it first located in your very core...then surrounding you, light touching every surface of your body...then expanding outward to encircle each woman near you. Watch as the flame dances and leaps, as an unseen breeze swirls around it; and be aware that the flame and the wind are the presence of God's love.

Prayer: As the flame rises free with light and warmth, we receive the gift of life.

As the wind moves and dances round the earth, we receive the gracious gift of the spirit. Amen.

—Prayer by Dorothy McRae-McMahon,[2]
Guided Meditation by Gail Ricciuti

SONG

"Spirit," *The Presbyterian Hymnal*

HEARING THE WORDS OF THE HOLY

John 3 NRSV (selected verses)

The following excerpts need not be printed in the order of worship but are included here to delineate the selection from John 3 for use by a reader.

Jesus answered [a questioner named Nicodemus], "Very truly, I tell you, no one can see the kingdom of God without being born from above." Nicodemus said to him, "How can anyone be born after having grown old? Can one enter a second time into the mother's womb and be born?" Jesus answered, "Very truly, I tell you, no one can enter the kingdom of God without being born of water and Spirit. What is born of the flesh is flesh, and what is born of the Spirit is spirit. Do not be astonished that I said to you, 'You must be born from above.' The wind blows where it chooses, and you hear the sound of it, but you do not know where it comes from or where it goes. So it is with everyone who is born of the Spirit."

AND HEARING THE HOLY WORDS OF WOMEN

Again, the following excerpts are printed only for use by individual readers.

The authors Sherry Ruth Anderson and Patricia Hopkins, having made a commitment to write a book about the unfolding of women's spirituality in individual lives, give this account of the beginnings of their project:

Two weeks later [after agreeing to work together] we were on our way to a cabin in the northern California redwoods, a place remote enough for us to concentrate fully on writing the first draft of the proposal for the book.... Once we had arrived at our cabin and settled in a bit, we stared at each other. "Now what?" we asked. Then, because we hadn't the faintest notion of how to answer that question, we walked outside and sat down opposite each other under the protective branches of a large oak tree. And there we did something we were to do almost every day for the next several years of our collaboration: We closed our eyes, sat in silence, and waited.

After a few moments, when we felt peaceful and in harmony with each other and our surroundings, Sherry asked the question that was on both our minds. "What is needed now?" And out of the silence came an answer with such calm and wisdom that we felt it was a voicing of the deep purpose that had brought us together. "Writing the proposal will not be hard work." I spoke the words as I was hearing them, and we were cautioned against forcing ourselves. Whenever we started to feel anxious and pressured to produce, we were to stop and go for a walk in the redwoods or along the river. If we were willing to do this, what was needed would come to us.

We discovered that this kind of communion was easy, and from the beginning it became an integral part of our process. We had not called upon the sacred by a particular name, but with open, trusting hearts. And perhaps equally important, we expected an answer. In the months that followed we found that this loving, knowing consciousness was present not only when the two of us sat together but later as well, during the few moments we would sit in silence with each of the women before beginning our interview.

...If women are to pioneer a new way of embodying spirit in the world today, one thing seems certain: we must listen to the deep source of wisdom within ourselves and tell the truth about our lives and what we are learning. This means questioning everything we have been taught or taken for granted that is not validated by our own experience. Simply by asking one key question, *Is this true for me?* about each "truth" we hear, we challenge ourselves to become what we truly are.

One woman told us about a circle of grandmothers who had come to her while she was on a retreat in the desert. "It was a time of great uncertainty in my life, and I prayed and listened more deeply than I ever had before. On the third day, I lit a small fire and began to

dance following the rhythm of my heartbeat. As I did this, I felt I
was being encircled by a ring of ancient, brown-skinned women who
were blessing me. They were blessing my breasts and womb and legs
and belly, and praising my strength and beauty and courage. As my
eyes filled with tears of gratitude, they told me that I should not weep
because this was my birthright as a woman. "At one time every woman
was blessed in this way," they said, "so no one could be pulled off
her knowing by a man. The young ones knew they were whole and
connected to everything that lived because we elders sat in witness for
them, just as we're doing for you today."

—Sherry Ruth Anderson, Patricia Hopkins,
from *The Feminine Face of God*[3]

Also appropriate here is the voice of Frances Weaver, author and humorist,
describing the inception of "The Society for Tethered Flight," from the
tape *The Girls With the Grandmother Faces.*[4]

HOW ARE *WE* ACCESSIBLE TO THE SPIRIT?

*Worshippers are given ample time to write cinquain poems on the front cover of
their worship bulletins according to the following instructions. When the page is
folded along the guidelines and taped into the shape of a kite, the poem should
be visible on the front.*
　　A *cinquain* (a five-line stanza) is written this way:

* Line 1: Give a one-word title (which becomes the subject of the
  stanza) naming yourself in relation to the wind of God's Spirit.

* Line 2: Give two words to describe the first line.

* Line 3: Give three "action words" that speak about how you personally
  "catch the wind."

* Line 4: Create a phrase descriptive of the subject.

* Line 5: Summarize in one word.

Examples:

Sensor
Heart alert
Waiting, hollowing, thirsting
Sail in wind
Saint

—gar

Listener
Clear expression
Anxious, hopeful, heartened
Words that soar
Prophet

— rcm

Receiver
New directions
Opening, reaching, feeling
Fresh breeze
Lifted

— ddj

Wing
Angelic, sere
Sensing, tensing, soaring
Abandoned to laughter
Untethered

— gar

SONG

For listening . . . or singing along . . .

Flow with the Winds of Spirit

CHORUS:
Flow with the winds of Spirit
Go with the winds of change
No need to resist or fear it
When your soul's being rearranged

It's time to release
What's between you and your peace
Let the winds of conflict cease
End your pain

CHORUS

The breezes that are blowing
Have a funny way of knowing
Where you need to do your growing
So they blow the change your way
And it's OK

CHORUS

All of the changes
Are moving you where you most want to be
You may not believe it
But your past is not your destiny

—Scott Kalechstein and choir and band
of Pebble Hill Church, an Interfaith Community
in Doylestown, Pa. Kathryn Cokkinos, vocalist[5]

SHARING OUR VISIONS

After the song is played or sung, whoever wishes to read her cinquain aloud is invited to do so, followed in each case by a group response: a deep breath and a long sigh, in unison!

NAMING AN "EARTH ANCHOR": A Tail in the Spirit Gale!

"Earth Anchor" refers to the essential tail of the kite, which keeps it stable in wind and counterbalanced gracefully. Each woman takes a streamer from the edge of the table and finds a partner. Each then names her own particular "anchor" to the other woman — the concern or issue or challenge in life for which she especially seeks the Spirit's presence. The partner tapes the tail to her kite, with the blessing "Fly free, sister of the Spirit!" and then takes a turn at naming her own "anchor." As these blessings are exchanged, the music that opened the service gradually rises as an ending benediction.

NOTES

1. Lighting of Candles litany was adapted from *The Iona Community Worshipbook,* © 1988 by Iona Community/Wild Goose Publications, Pearce Institute, 840 Govan Road, Glasgow G51 3UT, Scotland.

2. Invoking the Spirit litany is adapted from "Spirit of Joy" by Dorothy McRae-McMahon, Uniting Church in Australia, 222 Pitt Street, Sydney 2000 Australia (used with permission).

3. Excerpt from *The Feminine Face of God* © 1991 by Sherry Rochester and Patricia Hopkins. Used by permission of Bantam Books, a division of Bantam Doubleday Dell Publishing Group, Inc.

4. "The Inception of the Beulah Valley Society for Tethered Flight," from the book and tape *The Girls with the Grandmother Faces,* © 1987 by Frances Weaver. The tape can be ordered from The Publishing Mills, P.O. Box 481006, Los Angeles, CA 90048 (1-800-72-AUDIO)

5. "Flow with the Winds of the Spirit" by Scott Kalechstein from the album *Back to the Garden,* © 1990 SCOTTSONGS. Available through Pure Light, Box 189 Sea Cliff, NY 11579.

SUGGESTED ALTERNATE HYMNS

"Filled with the Spirit's Power" (LBW, UMH)

"Holy Spirit, Truth Divine" (vs. 1–3 in HB, MH, PH, UMH; vs. 1–4 in LBW, TPH, WB)

"Like the Murmur of the Dove's Song" (TPH, UMH)

"Loving Spirit" (TPH, vs. 1, 2, 4)

"Spirit of God, Unleashed on Earth" (LBW, TPH)

"The Lone Wild Bird" (HB, TPH, WB)

"Wind Who Makes All Winds That Blow" (UMH)

"Through Our Fragmentary Prayers" (NHLC)

8

SHE WITH THE FLOW OF BLOOD: A WOMEN'S SERVICE OF EMPOWERMENT

(Ordinary Time)

INTRODUCTION

Nothing is so much a testament to the inspiration of the Spirit in church history than that certain stories were ultimately retained in the canon. The story of the woman "who had a flow of blood for twelve years" is one such writing, offering a liberating word to women who would claim the beauty and worthiness of their own bodily selves.

Ancient teachings and the "collective unconscious" have too often convinced us that our female bodies and their functions and cycles, such as menstruation, are unclean. The law of Leviticus (see 15:19–31) emphasizes not only that a menstruating woman is unclean herself, but pollutes everyone and everything she touches. Even *Christian* authorities have held the same prejudices: In the thirteenth century, the Synod of Wurzburg ruled that no one should come near a woman during the time of her monthly flow; and as late as the seventeenth century, menstruating women were still forbidden to enter a church. (And of course women who had given birth were forbidden to enter any church for forty days, since they were also considered unclean for that time after the birth process.)

The original meaning of the word "taboo" was in fact "sacred." Women's ability to bleed without dying and to give birth was seen in ancient goddess-conscious cultures as sacred; but when men began to fear such power, the meaning "sacred" was changed to "forbidden."

It is stunning to realize the great courage shown by this "hemorrhaging" woman in having the nerve to *overcome* taboo and push through the crowd, thereby making others — including Jesus himself — unclean. The question arises: Is *this* moment "the faith that makes [her] whole"? Is it in *break-*

ing taboo that "your faith has healed you"? To one who has exhausted her resources on physicians and authorities who did not help her, Jesus gives her power back (*"Your* faith has healed you"), knowing that we so often attribute our power to others outside ourselves.

This Jesus is not a rescuer but a reminder. As Elisabeth Moltmann-Wendel observes (in *The Women around Jesus*), the woman has involved him in her fate: She becomes clean, and he becomes (ritually) unclean. Yet he does not berate her for this trespass, but rather affirms the liberation that she experiences physically. Only in Mark's Gospel is it noted that "she felt in her body that she had been made whole," and that wholeness/*shalom* is not only a bodily healing but her restoration to full community.

As we have experienced in worship, time after time, this celebration carried a power far beyond itself that spread in concentric circles through many women's lives. One participant happened to bring her eleven-year-old son with her to the gathering and was grateful that he had the opportunity to experience the moment when he too received a red sash with the charge, "Your faith makes you whole, my brother; and all of you is holy."

A few days later, one of us called upon an elderly woman of the congregation who had had major abdominal surgery the morning after this service. She pointed to the nightstand next to her hospital bed, on which there lay one of the red sashes carefully folded. Words of blessing had been lettered on it in black pen. "My daughter brought me one of your stoles the night before my surgery," she said with a smile, "and she told me all about the blessing that came with it, and put it around me. It was very comforting, and I stopped feeling afraid." In our worship, when it is authentic to our lives, lies not only our liberation but our empowerment to care for one another and the whole world.

PREPARATION

Advance planning for this Service of Empowerment includes the preparation of several dozen "stoles" or sashes of red cotton fabric, 36 to 48" in length and approximately 4" in width — numbering more than the estimated attendance at the service. The circle of chairs arranged for the celebration is centered upon a small, round pedestal-type table, over which two-thirds of the stoles are draped so that they "flow" to the floor. The table holds a large, round ceramic pitcher with the ends of the remaining stoles stuffed into it so that the red streamers "flow" out of the pitcher and over the edges of the table.

Red tapers are arranged on the periphery of the worship area to be lit during the service.

The passage to be read for Gathering the Community (see below) may be printed in bold type on the bulletin cover, as a focus for the celebration. Gospel passages parallel to Mark 5:24–34 should be copied from

Gospel Parallels and printed or inserted in the order of worship, for use in discussion.

With this service we instituted the opportunity for a free-will offering (with offering baskets near the entrance) designated on each occasion for a different community project ministering to women. Appropriately, the offering from this gathering was contributed to a local battered women's shelter.

❁

OPENING WORDS

How might it have been different for you if, on your first menstrual day, your mother had given you a bouquet of flowers and taken you to lunch, and then the two of you had gone to meet your father at the jeweler, where your ears were pierced, and your father bought you your first pair of earrings, and then you went with a few of your friends and your mother's friends to get your first lip coloring;

> and then you went,
> for the very first time,
> to the Women's Lodge,
> to learn
> the wisdom of the women?

How might your life be different?

—Judith Duerk,
from *Circle of Stones*[1]

HYMN

"When Twilight Comes," *The Presbyterian Hymnal*
To be sung twice

PRAYER

Leader: We all bleed.

All: We bleed for ourselves — we each have our private pain.

Leader: We bleed for others; and we bleed for a wounded world.

All: If we did not bleed for others
at some times and in some measure,
would we not be spiritually barren?
Unfit for our calling.
Incapable of conceiving and nurturing new life,
in forming relationships and caring communities?

Leader: But if the pain takes over, the bleeding becomes constant,
do we not then find
that we have lost touch with our God —
who is obscured by the crowd of our concerns —
the crowd of our activities —
perhaps even the crowd of our own words?

All: Holy One, help us to touch you now,
to lay before you our own, and the world's pain.
Help us as we wait in silence to feel your hands upon us.

— Janet Morley, from "Celebrating Women"[2]

THE READING OF HER STORY

Mark 5:24–34

CANDLELIGHTING

As the Music for Reflection begins to play, several women representing the diversity of the community (multiracial, younger and older, of varying lifestyles and orientations, for instance) rise to light the tapers on the periphery of the room.

MUSIC FOR REFLECTION

"Shalom Bells," from Dances of Universal Peace[3]

A TIME OF CONVERSATION

A leader invites reflection by the whole group, for five to ten minutes, upon the first question:

* What was it that healed her?

Worshippers are now invited to move their chairs into groups no larger than five or six and to converse together for the next twenty minutes on the following questions, using the printed gospel parallels as a resource:

* What community do you feel excluded from?
* What "taboo" do you need to break through in order to be whole?
* What do you get in touch with (or what do you touch) that gives you power? That is, what is *your* healing Source?

REFLECTIONS BY WORSHIP LEADERS

Leaders call the community back together with some thoughts on ancient attitudes toward women and "taboo" and then elicit sharing from representatives of the smaller groups, who are invited to list some of the taboos that participants recognize the need to break.

A WOMAN'S PSALM

Note that voices will divide according to age during this responsive psalm.

All: Holy the blood poured out for me
as a testament of love,
a pledge of faith,
a reconciliation.
Holy the blood that comes into me
through the cup of a new covenant,
the cup of my salvation.

Women over fifty:

Holy the blood that flows through me,
the blood of life,
my mother's blood,
my grandmother's blood,
the blood of her mother's mother
and the lineage of generations.

Women under fifty:

Holy the blood spilling out of me,
cleansing flood,
liberating blood.
A woman's blood is holy.

All: A bleeding woman images Christ
and all of her
is holy.

Blood is the symbol of death to life.
we thank you and praise you, life-giving God.

—Miriam Therese Winter,
WomanWord (adapted)[4]

RITUAL OF BLESSING

After giving directions for the ritual, two leaders approach the table and each lifts a red sash from the pitcher, then ties it around the waist or hips (or places it over the shoulders) of any member of the community. Those two, in turn, remove a sash and place it on two more women, and so on until everyone in the room has been blessed with a symbolic red sash and these words:

Your faith makes you whole, my sister; and all of you is holy.

UNISON PRAYER

Blessed are You, Holy One Who Bleeds.
You set Your seal irrevocably on the female enterprise.

You share Your deepest secret, the mystery of fecundity,
    with those who are bound by blood to You
    in a covenant of love.
May we not take this privilege lightly,
    but may we always cherish the gift so uniquely ours.
Protect us against all violence from outside or within,
    and keep us free to choose our grace
    from all You so graciously offer every day of our life.
Amen.

—adapted from Miriam Therese Winter,
Woman Word

SONG

Sing of a Blessing

The hymn may either be played on tape or led by one person who sings each phrase to be echoed by all participants together.

1. Sing, we sing of a blessing...
  A blessing of love...
  A blessing of mercy...

2. Pray now, pray for a blessing...
  A blessing of joy...
  A blessing of justice...

3. Share now, share in a blessing...
  A blessing of hope...
  A blessing of courage...

4. Live, live, live as a blessing...
  A blessing within...
  A blessing among us...

5. Send forth, send forth a blessing
  A blessing to all...
  Now and forever...
  Love will increase...
  A blessing of peace.

—Miriam Therese Winter,
WomanPrayer/WomanSong[5]

NOTES

1. Gathering Words by Judith Duerk from *Circle of Stones,* © 1989 by LuraMedia, Inc., San Diego, CA 92121.

2. Prayer by Janet Morley from *Celebrating Women,* published by Women in Theology, Holy Trinity House, Orsett Terrace, London W2 6AH, England, © 1986.

3. "Shalom Bells," from album *Creation Dances!* © 1990 Peaceworks Center for the Dances of Universal Peace, P.O. Box 626, Fairfax, CA 94930.

4. "A Woman's Psalm" and Unison Prayer by Miriam Therese Winter from *WomanWord: A Feminist Lectionary and Psalter,* © 1990 by Crossroad Publishing Co., 370 Lexington Ave., New York, NY 10017.

5. "Sing of a Blessing," by Miriam Therese Winter from *WomanPrayer/ WomanSong,* © 1987 by Crossroad Publishing Co., 370 Lexington Ave., New York, NY 10017.

SUGGESTED ALTERNATE HYMNS

"At Even, When the Sun Was Set" (HB, MH, vs. 1–3, 5, 6; PH, vs. 1–3, 5, 6)

"Faith, While Trees Are Still in Blossom" (UMH)

"O Christ, the Healer, We Have Come" (LBW, TPH)

"Spirit of Faith, Come Down" (MH, UMH)

"There Is a Balm in Gilead" (HUCC, MH, TPH, UMH, WB)

"We Walk by Faith and Not by Sight" (TPH)

"Woman in the Night" (UMH)

"Blest Be the Tie That Binds" (TPH)

9

SALTED AND HOLY

(Ordinary Time)

INTRODUCTION

"But Lot's wife, behind him, looked back, and she became a pillar of salt." It is the only mention of the wife of Lot in Scripture; yet it is the one detail of his story that has endured, larger than life, and is used against us early as a Sunday school lesson on what happens to those who "disobey God."

Curious about the strange event, we went back to approach the Genesis narrative using a simple discipline that can draw out so much of the Bible's richness: reading it *as if for the first time.* How would it have felt to be in her skin — suddenly to be saying goodbye to a town that, for all its profane tawdriness, nevertheless had always been "home"? The place where "I nursed my father . . . the night he died" and where my bread sometimes burnt, just like my neighbors' . . . To pack up and leave at a moment's notice would be painful enough, but never to look back at the roaring conflagration would be an inhuman effort, impossible for anyone with a heart. Abraham himself came early the next morning and gazed long toward the smoldering ruins, with no recorded ill effects.

What was it, then — what was the key to the mystery of the woman's apparent punishment? Suddenly, in our process of reading without preconception, the stunning realization dawned and was confirmed by our *own* tears that could not be held back: The text does *not* say that God punished her, that the Holy One turned her into a pillar of salt, as has so often been interpreted to us from childhood! Rather, " . . . she *became* a pillar of salt." Entering into her experience, understanding it in light of our own rites of passage and departures from "home," we finally comprehended how a broken-hearted woman standing at the outskirts of little Zoar could weep so strongly that she *became* her salty tears.

The ancient symbol of punishment is transformed to a metaphor of compassion in the bearing of this noble, nameless woman; and the image evokes scenes of Another, gazing across the Kidron valley and weeping for Jerusalem: the Jesus who taught that *we* are the salt of the earth.

That Lot's wife might be a profound model for our own moral compassion is borne out not only in Jesus' words and actions but in the ancient reverence for salt as a symbol of purification and rebirth. Its taste is like blood and seawater, both identified with the sacredness of the womb.

Nearly all Middle Eastern cultures used salt to consecrate altars and sacrifices and to repel demons. And from early Christian history, salt has been commonly used to "bless" altars and religious articles, as well as to bless a home before a family occupies it.

PREPARATION

How does one create a symbol of a woman-turned-to-salt? The power of the tangible symbol used in this service is well worth the additional effort involved: From a farm supply or feed store, purchase four salt licks (fifty-pound salt blocks) of the kind used to supplement cattle diets. (Afterward, ours were donated to an Amish farm in the area.) These are stacked, one on top of the other, in the center of the worship area and should be stabilized on a wooden base if the floor is carpeted (short lengths of two-by-fours work well) to guard against the possibility of toppling and causing injury.

Over the pillar is draped a several-yard length of sheer fabric to create the illusion of a human form, the traditional dress of a Middle Eastern desert woman. While the salt pillar remains slightly visible through the drapes of gauzy fabric, the "face" itself is left bare. A small (desktop size) electric fan may be directed at the form from some distance away, to create the slight movement of desert "breeze" through her garment.

Two small pedestals or pedestal tables stand slightly behind the pillar of salt, one holding a bowl of water and the other a bowl of coarse kosher salt. Chairs are arranged in two banks of semicircle rows facing each other, with the salt pillar in the center.

For greatest effectiveness within the service, the canon "By the Waters of Babylon" should be taught and practiced before worship begins: several times in unison, and then divided into parts.

At the end of the service the reader will find notes for adapting it for a conference setting that includes the Lord's Supper (see p. 89).

Worship begins starkly with two voices reading the Scriptures without introduction.

❀

OPENING SCRIPTURES

Genesis 19:1–11, 15–26; Luke 19:41–44

REFLECTIONS: THE PAIN OF WHAT SCRIPTURE HIDES

A leader reflects upon the traditional interpretation of the story: the background of Lot as righteous, in light of his offer to sacrifice his daughters, and the meaning of his wife's "punishment" and moves on to corporate reflection on feelings we've experienced when we have left — a hometown, a home, a relationship, a job, a college community — and turned to look back.

READING

The Pillar

Even to the nameless dog I said farewell.
Madness took him long since,
but I remember his sharp bark,
how he warmed my feet on cool evenings.
I nursed my father in that city,
raised a cup to his lips the night he died.
We laid him near the fig tree,
its twisted trunk his monument.
Now ash marks his place, and Mother's too,
and all the others whose bread sometimes burnt,
whose clay pots shattered, who wept with me.

They were not good people, and yet . . .
Lot's back was not enough to see.
I turned. One sign, one glance
for all we left behind.
My faith is strong —
yea, stronger even than salt.
I wait for God to forgive my love.

—Mary Cartledge-Hayes,
from *To Love Delilah*[1]

PRAYER OF CONFESSION (unison)

O God, we confess that we often look back.
We look back on mistakes we have made,
　　work left undone,
　　people we have hurt,
　　excuses we have made.
We see these as things for which we feel guilty.
We overwhelm ourselves with regret.

Free us, O God, from self-condemnation that immobilizes us.
Allow us to remember that you call us to look back.
　　To remember those times of joy.
　　To remember those people who were kind and compassionate.
　　To remember that we did the best we were able.
　　To remember that in Christ our past is transformed.
　　To remember that you journey with us each day of our life.
May we continue to grow in grace and truth,
in the name of Christ. Amen.

—Rosemary C. Mitchell

ASSURANCE OF GOD'S EMPOWERMENT

Leader: Please turn to someone near you and say: "Sister, may you
weep tears of redemption."

SONG

"By the Waters of Babylon," *The Presbyterian Hymnal*

RITUAL

*As worshippers sing the canon, each woman in turn walks to the center, dips two
fingers into the bowl of water, and then with those two wet fingers marks a trail
of tears on the face of the pillar of salt. Before returning to her seat, she touches
those fingers to her tongue, tasting the salty tears that are the only memorial to
Lot's wife. The singing ends when all have participated.*

READING

Maggid

The courage to let go of the door, the handle.
The courage to shed the familiar walls whose very
stains and leaks are comfortable as the little moles
of the upper arm; stains that recall a feast,
a child's naughtiness, a loud blattering storm
that slapped the roof hard, pouring through.

The courage to abandon the graves dug into the hill,
the small bones of children and the brittle bones
of the old whose marrow hunger had stolen;
the courage to desert the tree planted and only
begun to bear; the riverside where promises were
shaped; the street where their empty pots were broken.

The courage to leave the place whose language you learned
as early as your own, whose customs, however dan-
gerous or demeaning, bind you like a halter
you have learned to pull inside, to move your load;
the land fertile with the blood spilled on it;
the roads mapped and annotated for survival.

The courage to walk out of the pain that is known
into the pain that cannot be imagined;
mapless, walking into the wilderness, going
barefoot with a canteen into the desert;
stuffed in the stinking hold of a rotting ship
sailing off the map into dragons' mouths,

Cathay, India, Siberia, goldeneh medina,
leaving bodies by the way like abandoned treasure.
So they walked out of Egypt. So they bribed their way
out of Russia under loads of straw; so they steamed
out of the bloody smoking charnelhouse of Europe
on overloaded freighters forbidden all ports —

out of pain into death or freedom or a different
painful dignity, into squalor and politics.
We Jews are all born of wanderers, with shoes
under our pillows and a memory of blood that is ours
raining down. We honor only those Jews who changed
tonight, those who chose the desert over bondage,

who walked into the strange and became strangers
and gave birth to children who could look down
on them standing on their shoulders for having
been slaves. We honor those who let go of everything but freedom, who ran, who revolted, who fought,
who became other by saving themselves.

—Marge Piercy,
from *Available Light*[2]

CONVERSATIONS ON SALT: WHAT THE SCRIPTURE REVEALS

The circle is divided into small groups of three or four participants each. Each group is given an index card bearing one of the following texts, to be read aloud by one person in the group and then discussed for its positive images:

- Leviticus 2:13
- Numbers 18:19
- 2 Chronicles 13:5
- Colossians 4:5–6
- Matthew 5:13
- Mark 9:49–50
- Ezekiel 16:4

A leader might draw the discussions to a close by eliciting brief reflection from the whole community on the positive insights discovered in their conversations.

SONG

"Give to the Wind Thy Fears," *The Presbyterian Hymnal*

SALT OF HOSPITALITY

Each woman in turn comes forward to the pedestals and takes a pinch of salt. Returning to the neighbor on her right, she sprinkles it on the other's head, "salting" her with the blessing:

Have salt in yourself, my sister, and be at peace.

PRAYERS OF INTERCESSION

Individuals may be invited in advance to prepare prayers that they will voice in the following litany. At each response, the community sings the appropriate verses of "Here I Am, Lord" from The Presbyterian Hymnal

Voice 1:	[prayers for others]
Response:	"Here I Am, Lord" (verse 1 and chorus)
Voice 2:	[prayers for our church]
Response:	"Here I Am, Lord" (verse 2 and chorus)
Voice 3:	[prayers for our world]
Response:	"Here I Am, Lord" (verse 3 and chorus)
Voice 4:	[prayers for ourselves]
Response:	"Here I Am, Lord" (chorus)

BLESSING

Leader:	Jesus fixed his eyes on his disciples and said, "Blessed are you that weep now, for one day you will laugh.
People:	May our tears be the sign of our strength and compassion. May our laughter be the beacon of our liberation.
Leader:	May Her blessing remain with you always.
People:	May we walk on holy ground.

—Gail Ricciuti

SONG

"Blessing Song," Miriam Therese Winter, *WomanPrayer/WomanSong*

ADAPTATION WITH COMMUNION

The following adaptation, which was used for a Synod-wide women's conference, is also useful in settings that do not allow for much movement of participants and/or in situations in which blocks of salt cannot be procured.

For communion, worshippers are invited to come forward to one of several "stations" and partake by means of intinction. Three servers stand at each communion station — one with bread, one with a chalice, and one with a tray containing small cloth bags of salt. After receiving the sacrament, each worshipper is given a symbolic bundle of salt. (Directions for making such bags may be found on p. 89.)

A sermon or homily properly precedes the sacrament. (For reference, the sermon "Salted and Holy" by Gail Ricciuti may be found in *The Bible in Theology and Preaching* by Donald K. McKim, forthcoming from Abingdon Press.

WE INVOKE GOD'S PRESENCE, EACH IN OUR OWN WAY

For the call to worship, names of God are offered up simultaneously from the people of God.

    Leader: God of a thousand names and faces, at this moment in time we call you:

    Unison: _____.

    Leader: We your people of a thousand names and faces
                    now take this moment in time
                    to respond to you, O God,
                    as you have reached out to us.

    Unison: Come, let us celebrate together.

HYMN

"O Lord, Our God, How Excellent," *The Presbyterian Hymnal*

SCRIPTURE READING

Genesis 19:1–11, 15–26

A REFLECTION

"The Pillar," from *To Love Delilah*

SOLO RESPONSE

"By the Waters of Babylon"

ASSURANCE OF GOD'S EMPOWERMENT

All turn to someone near them and say:

                Sister, may you weep tears of redemption.

SCRIPTURE REPRISE

Genesis 19:15–29

SERMON

SOLO

"Turn Around, Take Time to Notice," by Kathy and Robert Eddy[3]

CELEBRATION OF THE LORD'S SUPPER

COMMUNION HYMN

"Give to the Wind Thy Fears," *The Presbyterian Hymnal*

After receiving communion, all receive a bundle of salt. Each is tied with red yarn, symbolizing the blood of women and of Christ, both shed for others. The red yarn is also the symbol of the International Decade of Churches in Solidarity with Women. The bundle of salt itself stands for the salt of women's tears — of pain, frustration, compassion, hunger, and abuse — throughout the ages and around the world. May it be a reminder that we who are able will act on behalf of our sisters who weep.

HYMN AFTER COMMUNION

"Let Us Talents and Tongues Employ," *The Presbyterian Hymnal*

BLESSING

❁

NOTES

   1. "The Pillar," by Mary Cartledge-Hayes, from *To Love Delilah,* © 1990 by LuraMedia, Inc., San Diego, CA 92121.
   2. "Maggid," from *Available Light* by Marge Piercy, © 1988 by Middlemarsh, Inc. Reprinted by permission of Alfred A. Knopf, Inc., New York.
   3. "Turn Around, Take Time to Notice," words and music by Kathy and Robert Eddy, Quaker Hill Press, Randolph, VT 05060

DIRECTIONS FOR SALT BAGS

Cut 4″ squares with pinking shears from scraps of fabric of many weights, textures, colors, and patterns. Place a heaping teaspoon of salt in the center of each square. Pick up the four corners and tie the "bag" with the red yarn — as close to the salt as possible. Vary colors and designs when placing the bags on trays for distribution. The variety of bags represents the different colors, personalities, and physical make-ups of women all over the world.

SUGGESTED ALTERNATE HYMNS

"Guide Me, O Thou Great Jehovah" (HB, HUCC, LBW, MH, PH, TPH, UMH, WB)

"If Thou but Suffer God to Guide Thee" (HUCC, PH, TPH, UMH)

"Jesus, Thy Boundless Love to Me" (MH, vv. 1, 2; LBS, vv. 1–3; TPH)

"O Love That Wilt Not Let Me Go" (vv. 1–3 from: HB, MH, PH, TPH, UMH, WB)

"Shalom, Chaverim!" ("Farewell, Good Friends") (HUCC, TPH, UMH)

"When There Is No Star to Guide You" (NHLC)

10

"FAMILY VALUES," OR HOUSEHOLD OF FAITH?

(Ordinary Time)

INTRODUCTION

During the presidential election campaign of 1992, the concept of "traditional family values" was debated almost daily in the media and highlighted constantly in the religious arena. Yet many diverse communities of faith were wise enough to begin asking "which *kind* of family?" and "*whose* traditional values?" The biblical idea of family encompasses tremendous variety! At least *forty* diverse forms of family are mentioned or implied in the Hebrew and Christian Scriptures, as Dr. Virginia Ramey Mollenkott points out in *Sensuous Spirituality: Out from Fundamentalism* (Appendix B, pp. 194ff.). Least prevalent of all in the biblical witness is the image of "nuclear" family popularly portrayed as *the* Christian ideal in the 1950s.

With the realization that Scripture *and* our own varied families challenge us to a rethinking of our ethics for life in community, the following worship experience was developed. It is designed to examine the biblical idea of family and to allow participants the space to reflect together upon the many dwelling places in the household of faith.

PREPARATION

Participants enter a worship space with small groupings of chairs around coffee tables, on each of which stand three to five framed portraits or photos of "family" groupings, both traditional and nontraditional. These may be clipped from magazines and placed in frames, or participants may be asked ahead of time to bring with them framed, free-standing photos for use in the service.

The worship bulletin should include a family tree design sketched on the front or back cover, for use in the segment "Praying the Family Tree."

❀

SONG

> For the fruit of Your womb,
> For the bread of our lives,
> For Your hands in the earth we adore You;
> For the clear-running springs
> Flowing up from our hearts,
> Mother God, we sing praises before You!
>
> —Words and music by Gail A. Ricciuti[1]

SUGGESTED ALTERNATE SONG

"Ubi Caritas," a round used by the Taizé Community

WHO ARE MY FAMILY?
A READING FROM MATTHEW AND MARK

Narrator: Jesus returned to Nazareth,
              his hometown,
              and taught in the synagogue
              on the sabbath.
              Those who heard him were astonished.

All: "Where did this man get his wisdom?
              Isn't he the carpenter's son?
              Isn't his mother the woman named Mary?
              Aren't James and Joseph and Simon and Jude
              his brothers?
              Aren't all his sisters living here with us?
              Then where did he get all this?"

Narrator: They simply could not accept him.
              And Jesus said to them:

Jesus: "Prophets are only rejected
              in their own neighborhood
              and in their own house."

Narrator: And he did not work many miracles there,
              because they did not believe.
              One day, while he was teaching,
              his mother and his brothers and sisters arrived,
              and they waited for him outside.
              A messenger told him,

All: "Your mother and brothers and sisters are here,
              and they are asking for you."

Narrator: Jesus said:

Jesus: "Who are my mother
and my brothers
and my sisters?"

Narrator: And looking at those all around him,
he said:

Jesus: "Here are my mother
and my brothers
and my sisters!
Whoever does the will of God
is my brother
and my mother
and my sister."

—Miriam Therese Winter,
from *Woman Word*[2]

SONG

"Part of the Family," words and music by James K. Manley[3]

The following readings are not printed in the order of worship, but are provided to individuals who read them aloud. The "musical interludes" are taped music for listening. The first interlude, "Sweet Betsy from Pike," is played in the middle of the first reading where indicated.

FIRST READING

As Presbyterians we affirm the centrality of family for church and society. We also recognize that family takes on many different forms from culture to culture and from age to age. We also acknowledge that the meaning of family is changing in our time, as it has in previous generations. Despite its various historical transformations from extended clan to modern nuclear family, from patriarchal hierarchy of ownership and control to egalitarian networks of mutual respect and care, family is valued. Family is valued precisely because it is an honored place for fulfilling God's purposes to enhance and protect intimacy and right-relatedness in the human community ...

Although many Christians in the post–World War II era have a special emotional attachment to the nuclear family, with its employed father, mother at home, and two or more school-aged children, that profile currently fits only 5 percent of North American households. Approximately one in six children now live in a single-parent, usually female-headed family. That pattern now represents 16 percent of all families in the United States ...

MUSICAL INTERLUDE

"Sweet Betsy from Pike," traditional American Ballad[4]

The diversity of family life is fascinating to many and alarming to others, especially those discomforted because there is no one family form that is statistically normative in this society. In addition to nuclear families, persons live, by choice or by circumstance, as single adults without children, as single parents with children, as couples living together or cohabitating, in same-sex unions with or without children, as childless couples or couples without children at home, as blended families . . . , as multigenerational or extended families, or as experimental families who claim familial ties among a tribe of friends and loved ones . . .

Not only should family life nurture and support our personal well-being, but it should also develop and strengthen the kinds of people who can be responsive to the gospel and to promote justice-love in all aspects of our lives. Families serve us well when they serve as primary locations for testing out and practicing a mature sexual ethic of empowerment for wholeness and responsibility.

—from "Keeping Body and Soul Together:
Sexuality, Spirituality, and Social Justice"[5]

SECOND READING

. . . the joy that isn't shared
I heard, dies young.

—Anne Sexton (1928–74)

Apart from my sisters, estranged
from my mother, I am a woman alone
in a house of men
who secretly
call themselves princes, alone
with me usually, under cover of dark. I am the one allowed in

to the royal chambers, whose small foot conveniently
fills the slipper of glass. The woman writer, the lady
umpire, the madam chairman, anyone's wife.
I know what I know.
And I once was glad

of the chance to use it, even alone
in a strange castle, doing overtime on my own, cracking
the royal code. The princes spoke

in their fathers' language, were eager to praise me
my nimble tongue. I am a woman in a state of siege, alone

as one piece of laundry, strung on a windy clothesline a
mile long. A woman co-opted by promises: the lure
of a job, the ruse of a choice, a woman forced
to bear witness, falsely
against my kind, as each
other sister was judged inadequate, bitchy, incompetent,
jealous, too thin, too fat. I know what I know.
What sweet bread I make

for myself in this prosperous house
is dirty, what good soup I boil turns
in my mouth to mud. Give
me my ashes. A cold stove, a cinder-block pillow, wet
canvas shoes in my sisters', my sisters' hut. Or I swear

I'll die young
like those favored before me, hand-picked each one
for her joyful heart.

— "Cinderella," by Olga Broumas[6]

MUSICAL INTERLUDE

"The Ones Who Aren't Here," words by John Calvi[7]

THIRD READING

A metaphor is an imaginative way of describing what is still unknown by using an example from present concrete reality. To say "I live in the 'Master's house'" is to provide a metaphorical description of one's position of subordination drawn from the concrete experience of women, servants, and children in many, many houses. To say "I live in a "household of freedom" is to use a metaphorical description of one's freedom to participate with others in a community of caring drawn from the concrete experience of the slaves living in Pharaoh's "house of bondage" and then moving out as the people of God toward a new "house of freedom."

— Letty Russell, from *Household of Freedom*[8]

CONVERSATIONS AROUND THE TABLE: HOW OUR MINDS HAVE CHANGED...

The following guide is printed in the order of worship. Participants are asked to fill out as much as they can, and then to use their reflections for conversation in small groups. A group may choose to focus on one of the categories for deeper discussion.

	I Used to Think...	But Now I Think...
Regarding marriage:		
Regarding parenthood:		
Regarding singleness:		
Regarding "faithfulness":		
Regarding friendship:		
Regarding "family":		

PRAYING THE FAMILY TREE

It is not necessary that prayer always be spoken. The following prayers are silent and visual and help worshippers to turn to God in a meditative mode of thanksgiving. Interspersing adequate silences in the manner of bidding prayers, the leader invites worshippers to reflect in God's presence and then to name onto their family tree (with pens or markers) the following persons:

  a. One not necessarily related to you by blood, whom you will always regard as "family" or spiritual kin;
  b. One you wouldn't have chosen but who reached out and chose *you;*
  c. One from whom you know you have something to learn;
  d. One who lives out her/his faith in a manner you wish to live yours;
  e. One not in your natural family that you (woman) regard as a *brother;*
  f. Another family member whom you particularly cherish as a gift from God in your life.

When these thanksgivings have been offered, a brief closing ascription of praise may be added by the leader to end the time of prayer.

A PSALM OF RELATIONSHIP WITH GOD

Worship bulletins should be highlighted ahead of time so that the leading voice(s) represent older, younger, middle-aged, multiracial individuals or groups within the gathered community.

Voice: Who is my mother, my sister?

All: Whoever does the will of God
is mother, daughter, sister.

Voice: Who is my mother, my sister?

All: Whoever does the work of God
is mother, daughter, sister.

Voice: Who is my mother, my sister?

All: Whoever keeps the word of God
is mother, daughter, sister.

Voice: Who is my neighbor?
Who is for me
my mother and my sister?

All: Whoever does the work of justice,
sits beside the wounded,
or ministers with compassion,
is our mother and our sister.

Voice: Who is God for me?
Is God really
my mother, my sister?

All: She Who knew you in the womb,
Who gave Her life to shield you
is Shaddai,
is Christa,
loving Mother,
risen Sister.

—Miriam Therese Winter,
from *Woman Word*[9]

BENEDICTION IN SONG

"Blest Be the Tie That Binds," *The Presbyterian Hymnal*

❁

NOTES

1. Original melody by Gail Ricciuti is included in the Resource Packet; see p. 18 for ordering information.

2. Reading from Matthew and Mark by Miriam Therese Winter from *Woman-Word: A Feminist Lectionary and Psalter,* © 1990 by Crossroad Publishing Group, 370 Lexington Ave., New York, NY 10017.

3. "Part of the Family" by Jim and Jean Strathdee on the album *Jubilee,* produced by Caliche Records; words and music © 1984 by James K. Manley. Tape can be obtained from James K. Manley, 2620 Huntington Dr., San Marino, CA 91108.

4. "Sweet Betsy from Pike," sung by Peg Lehman, is from her recording "What You Do with What You Got," lyrics adapted from traditional ballad by Andy Murray (public domain).

5. Excerpt from "Keeping Body and Soul Together: Sexuality, Spirituality, and Social Justice," a document prepared for the 203rd General Assembly, Presbyterian Church (U.S.A.), 1991.

6. "Cinderella" is from *Beginning with O,* copyright 1977 by Olga Broumas, vol. 72 of the Yale Series of Younger Poets, Yale University Press, New Haven and London.

7. "The Ones Who Aren't Here," written by John Calvi, from the album *The Best of Meg Christian,* Olivia Records, © 1990 John's Gay Music Co. B.M.I.

8. Excerpt from *Household of Freedom* by Letty Russell, © 1987 by Westminster Press.

9. "Psalm of Relationship with God" by Miriam Therese Winter from *Woman-Word: A Feminist Lectionary and Psalter,* © 1990 by Crossroad Publishing Group, 370 Lexington Ave., New York, NY 10017.

SUGGESTED ALTERNATE HYMNS

"God Made from One Blood All the Families of Earth" (NHLC)

"Help Us Accept Each Other" (TPH, UMH)

"How Firm a Foundation" (HB, HUCC, LBW, MH, PH, TPH, UMH, WB)

"We Need Each Other's Voice to Sing" (NHLC)

"Woman in the Night" (UMH)

11

REFORMATION WOMEN

(Reformation Sunday)

INTRODUCTION

Although seldom chosen as a text for the occasion, the story of the prophet Jeremiah at the potter's house is precisely the stuff of Reformation Sunday! For "whenever the vessel [she] was making came out wrong, as happens with the clay handled by potters, [she] would start afresh and work it into another vessel, as potters do." The church, like clay in a potter's hands, is wont to be pliant and unpredictable; lovers and reformers of the church, like the divine Potter who loves the House of Israel, must frequently "start afresh and work it into another vessel" if the result is to be both serviceable to this world and a work of art, evidencing the loveliness of justice.

Joy has been, consistently, one of the marks of this often-repeated celebration as we have carried it from our own community outward to conferences and other gatherings of women. Perhaps that joy springs not only from honoring the memory of sisters forgotten by the mainstream of history who were true mothers of the Reformation but also from the creative assertion in word, sculpture, and song that we too are the Reformation Women of our day. May it be so in every community that hears our sisters' voices ringing again through history and thereby finds a new voice of its own!

PREPARATION

The configuration of seating can vary greatly for this celebration, but the focal point remains the same whatever the arrangement of chairs: a large table, preferably long and rectangular and adorned with a colorful table runner, on which stands a simple church or cathedral structure ("minimalist" in design) constructed from bars of artist's clay. The clay can be purchased in one-pound packages containing four bars each from art suppliers, either in assorted colors or in basic gray. A minimum of one pound for every four women expected to attend (one bar per woman) should be used to build the stylized "church" in advance of the service. (Sixty women in attendance, for example, would suggest beginning with fifteen pounds — sixty bars — of clay. However, no matter how small the gathered community, we would suggest using no fewer than twenty bars or five pounds for the clay structure.)

99

Other items needed are a supply of small paper plates as bases for the final clay creations and a packages of wet-naps for hands rendered sticky from engaging in the work of "potters."

The words of the nine sisters of the Reformation do not appear in the order of worship but are printed out individually for use by nine readers.

❀

GATHERING

Psalm for Women-Church

Choir 1: Grace and peace be with you, sisters of Elizabeth and Mary.

Choir 2: Blessing and power of Spirit-church be with all women of God.

Choir 1: How good and wholesome and holy it is for women to come together.

Choir 2: We share our sacred stories,

Choir 1: sift through our graced experience and discover common ground,

Choir 2: create our creeds of courage and our paradigms of praise.

Choir 1: We hear one another into being,

Choir 2: laugh into life our sterile dreams, support the choice taking shape within us.

Choir 1: Women together share new life and celebrate miracles:

Choir 2: share how the barren bring to birth,

Choir 1: share the first fruits of believing,

Choir 2: share all the many and marvelous ways the Spirit impregnates women with the seeds of the new creation and the potential for significant change.

Choir 1: Old and young together,

Choir 2: ordinary women together break ground for a new world order that includes the fringe of society,

Choir 1: is rooted and grounded in justice

Choir 2: and grows strong in the embrace.

All: Our soul sings in the strength of Shaddai,
           our spirit rejoices in Her creation!

—Miriam Therese Winter,
Woman Word[1]

SONG

"Come Sing, O Church, in Joy!" *The Presbyterian Hymnal*

A READING FROM SCRIPTURE

Jeremiah 18:1–6

CALLING UPON THE SPIRITS OF OUR SISTERS
OF THE REFORMATION

The leader calls upon each of the nine women in turn, proclaiming in a ringing voice, "I call upon the spirit of Teresa of Avila!" etc. The appropriate reader then rises in place and tells her story. Where responses are inserted, the entire community reads the segments "We are Reformation Women..." in unison.

1. Teresa of Avila

I AM TERESA OF AVILA. I lived in Spain from 1515 to 1582. I became a nun at the age of sixteen, a Carmelite at twenty. I was a monastic reformer, a visionary, and according to some, one of the greatest mystic writers of all time. Although the Carmelites were fairly progressive, I always demanded higher standards; I reformed the order, and I established sixteen convents for women and fourteen religious houses for men. In addition to being a cloistered mystic, I became a capable businesswoman so as to better organize my order and protect it from powerful onslaughts. Admonishing my nuns to be disciplined and strong, I urged that their lives have purpose: I was always stressing that although convent life was difficult, it was better than being a wife! I also challenged the apostolic rule that forbade women to teach. I wrote my autobiography quickly and without erasures — "with abandon," some said. Perhaps that is why the Inquisition confiscated my manuscript! And perhaps that is why I wrote, "The very thought that I am a woman is enough to make my wings droop."

2. Katherine Zell

I AM KATHERINE ZELL. In sixteenth-century Germany, I was a zealous promoter of the Reformation and supporter of equality between women and men. I studied tracts written by Martin Luther, and he sent me a letter of congratulations on my wedding day. I published a collection of congregational hymns. I also cared for the sick and the imprisoned and the hordes of refugees who were displaced by religious warfare. When my husband died in 1548, I delivered the address after the eulogy. When my friend, the chief magistrate of Strasbourg, was stricken with leprosy, I wrote a little treatise of consolation that was later published. I also wrote a meditation on the Lord's Prayer and two simple catechisms for children; and in 1534 I issued a collection of hymns in the form of four pamphlets that sold for a penny apiece.

> *Response:*   We are Reformation Women.
> We claim our power.
> We proclaim our economic power.
> We are breadmakers and breadwinners.
> We affirm our responsibility
> to share the earth's goods with the earth's people,
> to build structures of economic justice for all.

3. Olympia Morata

I AM OLYMPIA MORATA, an Italian born in 1526. I was a distinguished classical scholar and a professor of philosophy; but since I was sympathetic to the Reformation, I was forced to take my unpopular religious views and move to Heidelberg. There, the University of Heidelberg offered me the professorship of Greek; but my brilliant career ended when I was overcome by the plague and died at the age of twenty-nine.

4. Vittoria Colonna

I AM VITTORIA COLONNA, who lived in Italy from 1492 to 1547. I am called the most influential woman of the Italian Renaissance, and I was considered Italy's greatest woman writer. My works dealt with many topics — among them, religion — and I was indeed concerned with religious reform. I was a friend of Margaret of Navarre and was also a friend and an inspiration to Michelangelo. He once wrote me: "Without wings, I fly with your wings; by your genius I am raised to the skies; in your soul my thought is born."

5. Argula Von Grumbach

I AM ARGULA VON GRUMBACH. I lived in Bavaria during the sixteenth century. Here is what you should know about me, and this will explain a lot: I led worship services in my home, conducted funerals without authorization, and — no surprise! — was imprisoned for my outspoken support of Luther.

> *Response:*   We are Reformation Women.
> We claim our power.
> We proclaim our spiritual power.
> We are healers and holy, priests and prophets.
> We affirm our responsibility to break bread
> and lift a cup in the name of liberation.

6. Mechthild of Magdeburg

I AM MECHTHILD OF MAGDEBURG. I lived in Germany to the ripe old age of eighty-seven, through most of the thirteenth century. Though I am known as one of the greatest religious figures of the Middle Ages, I am content simply to introduce myself as a mystic, a member of the Beguines. The Beguines were an order of laywomen devoted to charitable works. We were part of the reform movement and lived communally, supporting ourselves by nursing, weaving, lace making, and embroidery. The Beguines appealed particularly to single, independent women; and this was a good thing, since the authorities persistently attempted to discredit us as heretics! However, our order survived. I attempted to reform the decadence of the church in my age, and I was persecuted for my efforts. They charged me with (and I quote!) being "unlearned, lay, and, worst of all, a woman." Funny thing is, they were obviously right on at least two counts — and I claim my laity and my gender with pride! I was helped and protected by Gertrude the Great, who admired my writing, my courage, and, she said, my visionary powers.

7. Katherine Von Bora

I AM KATHERINE VON BORA. I left my convent to marry Martin Luther and to live with him in the house that formerly belonged to the Augustinian Friars. The marriage was not romantic, but it was solid! Centuries later, a male historian would write of me that I was "plain in features and unadorned in dress, but an excellent and busy housewife." (Wouldn't you just *expect* that from a male historian!) But at least I always spoke my mind. Martin was often outspoken himself, and even rude in his famous "table talks" on theology; and once I came right out and said to him, "Dear husband, you are too rude!" But he valued me, in his own lovable way: Once he wrote, "I would not change my Katie for France and Venice, because God has given her to me, and other women have much worse faults, and she is true to me and a good mother to my children."

> *Response:* We are Reformation Women.
> We claim our power.
> We proclaim our sexual power.
> We are moral agents who make decisions
> about our bodies.
> We affirm our responsibility to make choices
> that promote dignity and reflect love.

8. Queen Marguerite of Navarre

I AM QUEEN MARGUERITE OF NAVARRE, known as "the friend of reformers," and I lived in France from 1492 to 1549. It is said that I contributed more to the development of learning in France than any other individual of that time. I was patron of the arts and literature, and my salon became the stronghold of those who advocated and initiated the Reformation. In my spare time, I wrote a volume of religious poems and a collection of medieval tales.

9. Jeanne d'Albret

I AM JEANNE D'ALBRET, daughter of Margaret of Navarre, one of the Huguenots, born to her in 1528. Following in my mother's footsteps, I was scholar, poet, and religious reformer. As the Queen of Navarre, I withstood the Inquisition, which was invoked against me in 1563, and I established Protestantism throughout the country. New religious ideas were studied at my palace. In my free time, I worked a series of tapestries with religious liberty as their theme!

> *Response:*   We are Reformation women.
> We claim our power.
> We proclaim our political power.
> We are voters and change agents.
> We affirm our responsibility to
> influence public policy and to build a
> new world, starting with the struggling poor.

—Narratives by Gail A. Ricciuti,[2]
Responses by Mary E. Hunt[3]

CREATING OUR OWN "NINETY-FIVE THESES..." AND "POSTING" THEM!

The leader reminds those gathered of the symbolic event that is said to have begun the Protestant Reformation, using the basic summary that follows:

Martin Luther was in 1517 a thirty-three-year-old monk who was professor of Holy Scripture at the University of Wittenberg. For some years, he had been troubled over the doctrine and practice of selling indulgences, which were purchased by the faithful seeking remission of pains in purgatory.

Luther was pained greatly to hear that ignorant people were supposing themselves to have no further need of penitence because they had bought the indulgence — thinking they were, in a sense, "buying" forgiveness. The money was actually earmarked by the pope for the purpose of building St. Peter's in Rome.

On All Saints' Eve, October 31, 1517, Luther nailed to the door of the castle church at Wittenberg a placard inscribed with "Ninety-Five Theses upon Indulgences." He announced that he was ready to defend these at a public debate. Luther was not antipapal at the time and felt that if the pope actually knew what was happening he would rather see St. Peter's in ruins than built with the bones and flesh of his flock. The theses did not contain any of the central doctrines of the Lutheran Reformation; but this event is pointed to as marking the beginning of the Reformation.

Worshippers are then invited to come forward and dismantle the clay church by removing a bar of clay. Each finds a comfortable spot in the room — on a chair or on the floor — to create in clay a symbol of her deepest hope for what the church might become. Previous results have included both familiar and abstract symbols, butterflies rising from broken rocks, green shoots growing from hearts, hands clasped in friendship, figures dancing in circles. Often our sculpting fingers express a wisdom that our hearts cannot yet put into words! After at least fifteen or twenty minutes of time to work, worshippers are invited to bring their creations forward one by one and place them on the table with one word or phrase summarizing the hope expressed. Allow for movement around the table as women press closer to admire the astonishing images!

SONG

"One by One," from *WomanPrayer/WomanSong*[4]

THE BLESSING

❀

NOTES

1. "A Psalm for Women-Church" is from *WomanWord: A Feminist Lectionary and Psalter* by Miriam Therese Winter, © 1990 by Crossroad Publishing Co., 370 Lexington Ave., New York, NY 10017.

2. The words of the nine Sisters of the Reformation were written by Gail A. Ricciuti, using historical information drawn from the volumes *Women of the Reformation*, by Roland H. Bainton: *In Germany and Italy*, © 1971; *In France and England*, © 1973; *In Spain and Scandinavia*, © 1977 (Minneapolis: Augsburg Publishing House), and *The Dinner Party: A Symbol of Our Heritage* by Judy Chicago (Garden City, N.Y.: Anchor Press/Doubleday, 1979).

3. The litany used in "Calling Upon the Spirits of Our Sisters of the Reformation" is drawn from "Women-Church Proclamation" by Mary E. Hunt in *Prayers and Poems — Song and Stories, Ecumenical Decade 1988–1998*, "Churches in Solidarity with Women," 1988, World Council of Churches Publications, P.O. Box 2100, 1211 Geneva 2, Switzerland.

4. "One by One," by Miriam Therese Winter, is from *WomanPrayer/WomanSong*, © 1987 by Crossroad Publishing Co., 370 Lexington Ave., New York, NY 10017.

SUGGESTED ALTERNATE HYMNS

"Be Thou My Vision" (TPH, UMH, and vs. 1–3 in HB, PH, WB)

"Come Great God of All the Ages" (TPH)

"For All the Saints" (HB, HUCC, LBW, MH, PH, TPH, UMH, WB)

"Here I Am, Lord" ((TPH, UMH)

"How Clear Is Our Vocation, Lord" (TPH)

"I Sing a Song of the Saints of God" (HUCC, PH, TPH, UMH)

"O Master, Let Me Walk with Thee [You]" (HB, HUCC, LBW, MH, PH, TPH, UMH, WB)

"Open My Eyes That I May See" (HB, MH, TPH, UMH)

12

CELEBRATION OF THE CRONING OF VIRGINIA RAMEY MOLLENKOTT

(Born January 28, 1932)

INTRODUCTION

In 1992 Dr. Virginia Ramey Mollenkott, a dear friend and a distinguished author and theologian, requested that we create for her a service of croning to mark her sixtieth birthday — a passage into her "elder" years.

The title "Crone," as Barbara Walker points out in *The Woman's Dictionary of Symbols and Sacred Objects,* "once connoted an elder woman with the spirit of the Goddess within her."[1] Sadly, however, the name has come to have distressingly negative overtones in the modern West, attributing sinister motives to aging women. (It should be noted that the caricature of the Halloween "witch" bears no historical connection with the *wicca* who were the healers and herbalists of their time and worshippers of the Great Mother. Nor is the stereotype relevant to the tragedy of the millions of women in Europe and later of New England, who were put to death by the hysteria perpetuated by the church itself.)

Female elders "have generally been cursed with pejorative meanings in patriarchal society [but] there are still indications of their former spiritual authority," Walker writes. Just as the liberated church must reclaim designations like "evangelical," women of faith are also choosing to redeem — that is, to re-member the powerful meanings of — names like "Crone." The opportunity is ours to give thanks for the wisdom and experience of a ripening life by reverently conferring the title upon elder sisters who, like Virginia Mollenkott, have so faithfully pioneered the modern frontiers of spirituality and justice before us, and with us.

Our intention in including the celebration in this volume is that it may serve as a model for others — perhaps one day for every one of us in the faith community! — to be able to welcome and be grateful for advancing age. The service has been left specific: it is focused upon one woman and the particulars of her lifework to give some idea of how other similar celebrations might be developed. Every croning ceremony will be unique to the woman or women for whom the milestone is being marked.

The women of Congregation Ner Tamid of the South Bay (Rancho Palos Verdes, California) have written about the "Simchat Chochmah" ceremony they themselves created:

> It is a rite of passage which honors one of the many stages in life between the time of birth and the time of death. Like many other celebrations, [it] validates the part of life already lived, and empowers a portion of our future.... [It] marks the beginning of the Joy of Wisdom, the long-awaited reward of a full life.

Sarai (and Abram), Hagar, and Elizabeth, like others of our ancestors in faith, all were called into a new phase of their lives and spiritual journeys not in their youth, but when they were already advancing in age. In each case, we know little or nothing of their lives before this process of realization begins. But we do know that it was in their aging that they were called to take up the most monumental tasks.

Dr. Mary Daly, in her book *Webster's First New Intergalactic Wickedary of the English Language*, defines a crone as one "whose status is determined not merely by chronological age, but by crone-logical considerations; one who has survived early stages of the Otherworld Journey and who therefore has Dis-covered depths of Courage, Strength, and Wisdom in her Self."[2]

A croning celebration is an opportunity to redefine time and relationship in a new way, even as we redefine our culture's impoverished view of advancing age. The celebration therefore has a sacramental quality to it, in the sense of transforming common things to an uncommon and holy purpose.

PREPARATION

The service that follows was celebrated by eleven people and held in the living room of the honoree's home. Chairs encircled the room, with a small low table in the center that held a stoneware oil lamp whose wick had never been lit. Around the oil lamp stood small glass bowls of water, with floating candles (unlit) numbering one for each person present. On the hearth were stacked editions of all of Virginia Mollenkott's books (in all the languages in which they have been published) for use in the segment "Affirmation of the Maiden and Mother Phases of a Life's Work."

In creating the croning ceremony, it must be determined what are the proper, tangible symbols of the woman's life and accomplishment — her writings, or tools of her "trade," or other items symbolizing the work, artistry, and commitments in her life. These are ceremonially passed from hand to hand during the celebration.

The readings, which we have included here, are not intended to appear within the order of worship but to be read aloud by individuals. It is therefore necessary that they be printed out for use by individual readers.

❁

GATHERING THE CIRCLE

All: "When a woman feels alone,
         when the room is full of demons,"
         the Nootka tribe tells us,
         "the Old Woman will be there."

VRM: She has come to me over three thousand miles,
         and what does she have to tell me,
         troubled "by phantoms in the night"?
         Is she really here?

All: What is the saving word from so deep in the past?
         From as deep as the ancient root of the redwood,
         from as deep as the primal bed of the ocean,
         from as deep as a woman's heart sprung open again,
         through a hard birth or a hard death?

VRM: Here, under the shock of love,
         I am open to you, Primal Spirit,
         one with rock and wave,
         one with the survivors of flood and fire.

All: We have rebuilt their homes a million times,
         have lost their children, and borne them again.

VRM: The words I hear are strength, laughter, endurance.
         Old Woman, I meet you deep inside myself.
         There, in the rootbed of fertility,
         world without end, as the legend tells it,
         under the words, you are my silence.

                    —adapted from *Letters from Maine*, May Sarton[3]

We join hands and become quietly centered in Holy Presence, which also incorporates our presence to one another.

FLUTE REFLECTION

Of the [Mother's] Love Begotten
(ancient plainsong chant)

Of the [Mother's] love begotten,
Ere the worlds began to be,

[S]he is Alpha and Omega,
[S]he the source, the ending [S]he,
Of the things that are, that have been,
And that future years shall see,
Evermore and evermore!

THE LIGHTING OF THE CRONE FLAME: Virginia

The honoree lights the flame of the oil lamp.

THE COMING OF WISDOM'S LIGHT: John 1:1–5, 9, 12–13

In the beginning was Sophia, and Sophia was with God, and Sophia was God. She was in the beginning with God; all things were made through her, and without her was not anything made that was made. In her was life, and the life was the light of everyone. The light shines in the darkness, and the darkness has not overcome it . . .

The true light that enlightens everyone was coming into the world. . . .

[And] to all who received her, who believed in her essence, she gave power to become children of God; who were born, not of blood nor of the will of the flesh nor of human will, but of God Herself.

—paraphrase by Gail Ricciuti

PRAYER

Our Mother God, ancient crone coming to fullness in us;
may the flame of your love be our passion,
and Your waters of grace spring from the bedrock of our lives;
that we may offer healing to the world
as bearers of joy for all Your children.

—Gail Ricciuti

READINGS

From the Hebrew Scriptures: Wisdom 7:22–30, 8:1–2

For within her is a spirit intelligent, holy,
unique, manifold, subtle,
mobile, incisive, unsullied,
lucid, invulnerable, benevolent, shrewd,
irresistible, beneficent, friendly to human beings,
steadfast, dependable, unperturbed,
almighty, all-surveying,
penetrating, all-intelligent,

pure and most subtle spirits.
For Wisdom is quicker to move than any motion;
she is so pure, she pervades and permeates all things.
She is a breath of the power of God,
pure emanation of the glory of the Almighty;
so nothing impure can find its way into her.
For she is a reflection of the eternal light,
untarnished mirror of God's active power
and image of God's goodness.

Although she is alone, she can do everything;
herself unchanging, she renews the world,
and, generation after generation, passing into holy souls,
she makes them into God's friends and prophets;
for God loves only those who dwell with Wisdom.
She is indeed more splendid than the sun,
she outshines all the constellations;
compared with light, she takes first place,
for light must yield to night,
but against Wisdom evil cannot prevail.
Strongly she reaches from one end of the world to the other
and she governs the whole world for its good.

Wisdom I loved and searched for from my youth;
I resolved to have her as my bride,
I fell in love with her beauty.

From Women's Experience: "Alma Mater"

Through the years, from time to time, a woman walked through my day-dreams and night dreams. She also appeared in many paintings, stayed briefly and then vanished into the subcutaneous layer of content. Distant, always moving left, never looking at me, she glided through the landscape, robed, carrying many roses. I never saw her feet and for some reason this puzzled me.

Speaking to her, I began to call her Alma Mater, watching her, watching her strangely motionless passage. Then she appeared in a painting and stayed and I came to recognize her, a woman manifesting the journey into the crone moon, the journey into wisdom and regeneration. She does not need feet for she glides astride the body of the Serpent who is moving into its own phase of renewal, sloughing off a dead self, sliding out of an old mask.

—Meinrad Craighead,
The Litany of the Great River[4]

SINGING

Be Thou My Vision

Be thou my vision, the joy of my heart;
Nought be all else to me save that thou art.
Thou my best thought, by day or by night,
Waking or sleeping, thy presence my light.

Be thou my wisdom, the lamp to my feet;
Thy word, like honey, to my lips is sweet;
Thou my delight, my joy, thy command;
My dwelling ever, be the palm of thy hand.

—words adapted by Ruth Duck,
Everflowing Streams

SHARING HOPES FOR OUR AGING, AND THE ASSUMPTIONS WE REJECT

Friends are asked to voice both their greatest hope for their elder years and the cultural assumption about aging that they most strongly reject.

READING

The longer I live the more I mistrust
theatricality, the false glamour cast
by performance, the more I know its poverty beside
the truths we are salvaging from
the splitting-open of our lives.
The woman who sits watching, listening,
eyes moving in the darkness
is rehearsing in her body, hearing-out her blood
a score touched off in her perhaps
by some words, a few chords, from the stage:
a tale only she can tell.

But there come times — perhaps this is one of them —
when we have to take ourselves more seriously or die;
when we have to pull back from the incantations,
rhythms we've moved to thoughtlessly,
and disenthrall ourselves, bestow
ourselves to silence, or a severer listening, cleansed
of oratory, formulas, choruses, laments, static
crowding the wires. We cut the wires,
find ourselves in free-fall, as if
our true home were the undimensional
solitudes, the rift

in the Great Nebula.
No one who survives to speak
new language, has avoided this:
the cutting-away of an old force that held her
rooted to an old ground . . .

—Adrienne Rich, "Transcendental Etude"[5]

HONORING THE CRONES IN OUR LIVES

Each participant comes forward to name a "crone," living or gone ahead of us, whom s/he knew or not, who inspired her/his life significantly. Using a long fireplace match lit from the flame of the oil lamp, s/he lights one of the small floating candles.

As each lights this candle from the Crone Flame, s/he says,

I call upon the spirit of _____.

THE CRONING OF VIRGINIA

. . . in which the new elder receives her title, "Wise Woman," and a blessing.

AFFIRMATION OF THE MAIDEN AND MOTHER PHASES OF A LIFE'S WORK

One leader reads the phrases below — with long moments in between categories — while books are passed from hand to hand, several at a time.

One: Virginia, these books, which have so transformed our consciousness and even our broader society, symbolize the energy of your youth and middle years:

In social analysis . . .

All: May these sparks light an undying flame!

One: In literature . . .

All: May these sparks light an undying flame!

One: In theology . . .

All: May these sparks light an undying flame!

One: In spirituality . . .

All: May these sparks light an undying flame!

One: In poetry . . .

All: May these sparks light an undying flame!

One: In human relations . . .

All: May these sparks light an undying flame!

One: In interfaith understanding...

All: May these sparks light an undying flame!

One: In advocacy for justice...

All: May these sparks light an undying flame!

One: And in ethical discourse...

All: May these sparks light an undying flame!

One: We have passed them through our own hands to affirm how powerfully you have touched and molded every one of our lives; but we, who are few, represent a mighty cloud of witnesses.

COMMISSIONING OF THE CRONE

Certain folkloric sources remembered that the triangle was the sign of the Goddess as Wise Crone and gave that sign the title of Creative Intellect. After each of the following blessings voiced by the whole group, one celebrant at a time lays hands upon Virginia in this triangular sign of the crone and adds her/his own blessing, prayer, or words of empowerment.

All: Blessed is she who believed there would be a fulfillment of what was spoken to her by God.

One: I bless you, Virginia, Wise Woman.

All: May you be glad for the life you have chosen and look back upon the way you have journeyed with unutterable joy.

One: I bless you, Virginia, Wise Woman.

All: May you, a bright lodestar to others, discover the new thing God Herself will do through you in your crone years.

One: I bless you, Virginia, Wise Woman.

All: May you remain strong to confront injustice and powerful to rebuke the arrogant.

One: I bless you, Virginia, Wise Woman.

All: May you continue to feed the hungry of mind and heart and send away satisfied those who are empty.

One: I bless you, Virginia, Wise Woman.

All: May you give voice to the voiceless with renewed strength and courage to those in despair.

One: I bless you, Virginia, Wise Woman.

All: May you know the stamina of spirit that is rooted and grounded in love; and may your visions be fulfilled in company with us.

One: I bless you, Virginia, Wise Woman.

All: May you never be alone, but always supported in your struggle, and in every place find sisters and brothers standing with you.

One: I bless you, Virginia, Wise Woman.

All: May your years be long in the arms of your beloved Debra, rich with laughter and deepening joy; and may the covenant of your lives bring comfort and courage to all couples who dare to love.

Debra: I bless you, Virginia, Wise Woman.

All: May advancing age be in your eyes both blessing and gift; and may you anticipate without fear your crossing over to another life.

One: I bless you, Virginia, Wise Woman.

—Litany by Gail A. Ricciuti

PRAYER

Eternal wisdom, source of our being,
and center of all our longing,
in you our sister Virginia has lived to a strong age:
a woman of dignity and wit,
in loving insight now a blessed crone.
May the phase into which she has entered
bear the marks of your spirit.
May she ever be borne up
by the fierce and tender love of friends
and by you, most intimate friend;
and clothed in your light,
grow in grace as she advances in years;
for your love's sake. Amen.

—Gail A. Ricciuti

BLESSING THE COMMUNITY: Wise Woman Virginia

The new crone is invited in advance to prepare a final blessing to bestow on her friends.

OPENING THE CIRCLE

> *One:*   This circle has never been before and will never be, in just
>   the same way, again. As it is opened, let it truly remain
>   unbroken — that its blessing may extend to all whom we
>   touch as we journey on. So let it be!

SINGING

Sophia's Song

1. Sophia ever radiant and longing to be known.
   The seeds of all our freedom are eager to be sown.
   She is our vig'lant guardian if we will seek her love.
   Sophia may we find you in glory from above.

   REFRAIN:
   Wisdom of God,
   Wisdom of the ages.
   Illumine our path through the perils of night.
   Wisdom of our God, guide us in our journey.
   Warm and bright be the lamp's eternal flame.

2. So penetrate our spirit and permeate our lives.
   Be steadfast in our being, bring beauty to our eyes
   Our mother and our sister, our mentor and our friend.
   Help us in the struggle and lead us to the end.

   REFRAIN

                                                    —Alan Jones[6]

❋

NOTES

1. Excerpt from *The Women's Dictionary of Symbols and Sacred Objects,* by Barbara G. Walker, © 1988 by Barbara Walker. Reprinted by permission of HarperCollins Publishers, Inc.

2. Definition of "Crone" from *Webster's First New Intergalactic Wickedary of the English Language* by Mary Daly, conjured in cahoots with Jane Caputi, © 1987 by Mary Daly. Reprinted by permission of by Beacon Press.

3. Excerpt from *Letters from Maine* by May Sarton, © 1984 by W. W. Norton & Co., 500 Fifth Ave., New York NY 10110.

4. "Alma Mater" by Meinrad Craighead from *The Litany of the Great River,* © 1991 by Meinrad Craighead. Used by permission of Paulist Press.

5. "Transcendental Etude" by Adrienne Rich from *The Dream of Common Language: Poems 1974–1977* published by W. W. Norton & Co., Inc., 500 Fifth Ave., New York NY 10010. © 1978.

6. "Sophia's Song," words used by permission of author and composer, Alan Jones, Rochester, N.Y., © 1990. Music is included in Birthings and Blessings Resource Packet; see p. 18 for ordering information.

SUGGESTED ALTERNATIVE HYMNS

"Come My Way, My Truth, My Life" (LBW, UMH)

"Dow-Kee, AimDaw-Tsi-Taw" (Great Spirit I Pray to You) (UMH)

"Holy Spirit, Truth Divine" (vv. 1–3 HB, MH, PH, UMH; vv. 1–4 LBW, TPH, WB)

"Immortal, Invisible, God Only Wise" (vv. 1–3 HB, HUCC, LBW, MH, PH, TPH, UMH, WB)

"Like the Murmur of a Dove's Song" (vv. 1–2 TPH, UMH)

"Spirit" (TPH) "The Lone Wild Bird" (HB, TPH, WB)

"Wellspring of Wisdom" (HB, TPH, WB)

"Eagles' Spiralings Comply" (NHLC)

PART II

Celebrations for Inclusive Communities

13

THE RISK OF "RETURNING HOME"

(Christmas I)

INTRODUCTION

This service was planned for one of the Sundays between Christmas and Epiphany. The Jeremiah and the John texts both include pieces about "returning home." In John 1 we read the familiar words, "He came to his own home, and his own people did not receive him." It is a reference to that event in Jesus' life when he returned home and read from the book of the prophet Isaiah, giving new meaning to ancient words and thereby challenging tradition. His own people *did not receive him* and tried to kill him. Jesus' response was to move on. He spent his life with nowhere to place his head or to call home; yet he always extended a welcome to God's household, inviting others to be at home with God.

The Jeremiah passage describes the exiles returning home with joy. The prophet proclaims that God has rescued them, gathering them together from throughout the earth. They will come home so joyously that they will feel like a watered garden and will dance, celebrate and feel God's goodness. Life has been forever changed for them. What they return to cannot possibly be what they left: the place is changed and they are changed; but they are still together. They are now home at last! God welcomes them.

The two passages are opposite ends of a spectrum, symbolizing the experience of "returning home" for each of us. At one end returning home might get you killed (either physically or spiritually). But returning home *can* be an unbelievably joyous occasion — even if you have been through horribly traumatic times.

Many of us fall somewhere in between these two ends of the spectrum. For this service the worship leader may reflect on her/his own experience of "returning home" for Christmas (or returning home at any time). What comes to mind when we hear the words "returning home" — and what or where is "home" for each of us?

At the time of Communion the liturgy should include words about the welcome we each receive to the table and into the household of God.

PREPARATION

The room is arranged in two concentric circles with four aisles. Just outside the room a large Christ candle is burning. People enter by a nearby door where there is a welcome mat. (This service was originally held on a Communion Sunday, "in the round," and four welcome mats — each different — were positioned on the floor around the table.) The service begins with two different voices, one the voice in the wilderness and one the voice of Christ. The person who is the voice of Christ brings the candle into the room and places it near the table. At the beginning of the service, only the Communion Table is spotlighted; then during the Unison Prayer the lights are raised.

❀

THE CALL TO WORSHIP

A voice in the wilderness:

"Jesus came to his own home, and his own people did not receive him." (John 1:10)

The Light of Christ:

"Listen, I stand at the door and knock. If anyone hears my voice and opens the door I will come into that house. I will eat with those who live there, and they shall eat with me."

Leader: Come, Lord Jesus, be our guest, stay with us.
         Bring to our house your poverty,

All: for then we shall be rich.

Leader: Bring to our house your pain,

All: that, sharing it, we may also share your JOY.

Leader: Bring to our house your understanding of us,

All: that we may be freed to learn more of you.

Leader: Bring to our house all those
         who hurry or hesitate toward you,

All: that we may meet you as the friend and savior of all.

Leader: With friend, with stranger,
         with neighbor, and the well known ones,
         be among us this day,

> *All:*   for the door of our house we open
>   and the doors of our hearts we leave ajar.

—adapted from
The Iona Community Worshipbook[1]

THE LIGHT OF CHRIST ENTERS OUR HOUSE

The Christ candle is carried in.

SOLO

"Goin' Home"[2]

UNISON PRAYER

Creator, Word, and Holy Spirit, One God in perfect community.
Look now on us who look for you, the ever present and evasive One.
Here we ask for your care on this community:
Where there is falseness, smother it by your truth.
Where there is any coldness, kindle the flame of your love.
Where there is any resentment, replace it with trust and compassion.
Where there is anything we will not do for ourselves,
make us discontent until it is done.
And make us one, as you are one.

SONG

"O Word of God Incarnate," *The Presbyterian Hymnal*

WORDS ON THE RISKS OF RETURNING HOME

John 1:1–18 and Jeremiah 31:7–14

REFLECTIONS ON RETURNING HOME

At this point the worship leader offers some background on the passages and some personal reflections as well. The worshippers are invited to divide into groups of four or five for discussion of the following questions:

- Do we return with joy?

- Do we expect to be received?

SOLO

"Bring us Safely Home"[3]

CONCERNS OF THE COMMUNITY

OFFERING

PRAYERS OF THE PEOPLE

> *Response:* Christ is the source of life;
> Christ brings light to the world.

SHARING THE BREAD AND THE CUP

The Invitation

The Great Prayer of Thanksgiving:

Reminding us of the drama of Incarnation. That we might learn to be like God from our God who came to be like us.

The Words of Institution:

Recollecting the drama of Salvation. That we remember that we merely set the table; it is God who extends the invitation, and all are welcome.

The Lord's Prayer

The Gifts of God for the People of God and the Peace of Christ

CLOSING HYMN

"O Living Bread from Heaven"[4]

BLESSING

NOTES

1. The Call to Worship and the Unison Prayer are adapted from *The Iona Community Worship Book,* © 1988 by the Iona Community/Wild Goose Publications, Pearce Institute, 840 Govan Road, Glasgow G51 3UT, Scotland.

2. "Goin' Home" by Anton Dvorak (New World Symphony), words and adaptation by William Arms Fisher. Oliver Ditson Co., Theodore Presser Co., Bryn Mawr, Pa.

3. "Bring Us Safely Home," words by John Ylvisaker, tune in the public domain. From *Borning Cry,* vol. 1, published by Ylvisaker, Inc., Box 321, Waverly, IA 50677.

4. "O Living Bread from Heaven" is a song in the public domain. The authors found this song in *Borning Cry,* vol. 2.

SUGGESTED ALTERNATE HYMNS

"Blest Be the Tie That Binds" (HB, LBW, MH, PH, TPH, UMH)

"Draw Us in the Spirit's Tether" (HUCC, TPH, UMH)

"I Come with Joy" (TPH, UMH)

"O Gladsome Light" (HB, LBW, PH, TPH, UMH, WB)

"Where Charity and Love Prevail" (LBW, UMH)

14

ANALOG LIVES, DIGITAL LIVES

(*A New Year's Reflection*)

INTRODUCTION

It is the psalmist's insight that our time on earth is like the lifespan of mere grass in light of the entire sweep of chronological history. The subtle underlying theme of the following service, then, has to do with perspective on God's *kairos*. Psalm 90, often used in funeral liturgies, is unfortunately most often used to convey a misleading prescriptive message: "You sweep [us] away; [we] are like a dream, like grass that is renewed in the morning... in the evening it fades and withers." We *hear* the text to say, "This is how things are divinely ordained." The unfortunate result is a reinforcement of people's secret conviction of God's wrath.

Given that the Psalms are the prayerbook of the Bible, however, the authentic message of the psalmist — with potential to open our hearts to God's work in a new way — is "this [sense of transience] is how we so often *feel*." The message is strongly worded in order to make a point with us: that we have been so consumed with what we believe to be our own powers that we lose sight of the *true* power of the Spirit at work. The stark ticking of clocks, the calendar pages of our lives scattered across the floor like so many fallen leaves: These provide counterpoint to the message of grace that in God there is all the time in the world. "So teach us to number our days that we may get a heart of wisdom!"

PREPARATION

For this service, the worship space is arranged randomly with groupings of chairs in threes or fours around the room, interspersed with numerous small tables and pedestals holding clocks of all kinds. Worshippers are invited ahead of time to bring with them some sort of clock from home; and the resulting collection may include foreign varieties, heirloom or small grandfather clocks, mantle clocks, contemporary clocks, and ordinary wind-up alarms. Any clocks with alarms or gongs should be set at the beginning of the hour to strike randomly throughout the worship time — including at least one clock (ours was purchased specifically for the service, at minimal cost) of the old, raucous, "bell-on-the-top" variety that not only rings loudly but ticks like a time bomb. The floor is covered with randomly strewn individual sheets from a 6″ x 6″ page-a-day calendar purchased from any stationer. The calendar need not be a current one, but should have large numbers (preferably 3″) and show the day of the week and month of the year. One such calendar — 365 sheets — dismantled, should make more than enough of a "carpet" for the area.

For our service, the bulletin cover was an enlarged photo of the top of a parking meter, with the red flag through the window boldly announcing "Time EXPIRED."

❁

GATHERING WITH SONG

Be Still and Know
(composer unknown)

"Be still and know that I am God.
Be still and know that I am God.
Be still and know that I am God."

Alleluia! Alleluia! Alleluia!

"I am the Lord that strengthens you . . ."

In you, O Lord, I put my trust . . .

May be sung to the tune "Gelobt Sei Gott" or any other 8.8.8. meter with alleluias

CALLED TO WORSHIP BY THE TICKING

A time of centering.

HEARING THE WORD

Point out to participants that we will hear the Word in two ways: through the Scripture read aloud, but also through a contemporary poet's phrasing in song.

Psalm 90:1–12
(from the Inclusive Language Lectionary)

One: O God, you have been our dwelling place
         in all generations.
         Before the mountains were brought forth,
            or ever you had formed the earth and the world,
            from everlasting to everlasting you are God.

All: You turn people back to the dust,
             and say, "Turn back, O mortals!"
         for a thousand years in your sight
             are but as yesterday when it is past,
             or as a watch in the night.

One: You sweep people away; they are like a dream,

All: like grass which is renewed in the morning:

One: in the morning it flourishes and is renewed;

All: in the evening it fades and withers.

One: For we are consumed by your anger;

All: by your wrath we are overwhelmed.

One: You have set our iniquities before you,

All: our secret sins in the light of Your countenance.

One: For all our days pass away under your wrath,

All: our years come to an end like a sigh.

One: The years of our life are threescore and ten,
             or even by reason of strength fourscore;

All: yet their span is but toil and trouble;
             they are soon gone, and we fly away.

One: Who considers the power of your anger,

All: and your wrath according to the fear of you?

One: So teach us to number our days

All: that we may get a heart of wisdom.

SINGING THE WORD

"Lord, You Have Been Our Dwelling Place," *The Presbyterian Hymnal*

REFLECTING: The Perspective of a Psalmist

Here there is group discussion of the two "translations" of Psalm 90 that we have experienced:

- Which version speaks to you?

- What verse speaks directly to you, and why?

INTERLUDE: We Listen to the Ticking

After some moments of silence that is not really silence, but filled with the suddenly prominent ticking of the various clocks around the room, one voice (a capella or accompanied) sings the old favorite, "My Grandfather's Clock." The words are included here as background for the worship leader, but should not be printed in the order of service:

My grandfather's clock was too large for the shelf
So it stood ninety years on the floor.
It was taller by half than the old man himself
Tho' it weighed not a pennyweight more.
It was bought on the morn of the day that he was born
And was always his treasure and pride.
> REFRAIN:
> But it stopped short, never to go again
> When the old man died.

Ninety years without slumbering (tic toc, tic toc)
His life seconds numbering (tic toc, tic)
> REFRAIN

In watching its pendulum swing to and fro
Many hours had he spent as a boy.
And in childhood and manhood the clock seemed to know
And to share both his grief and his joy.
For it struck twenty-four when he entered at the door
With a blooming and beautiful bride.
> REFRAIN

Now my grandfather said that of those he could hire
Not a servant so faithful he found.
It wasted no time and it had but one desire
At the end of each week to be wound.
And it stayed in its place, not a frown upon its face
And its hands never hung by its side.
> REFRAIN

It rang an alarm in the dead of the night
An alarm that for years had been dumb.
And we knew that his spirit was pluming its flight
That his hour of departure had come.
Still the clock kept the time, with a soft and muffled chime
As it silently stood by his side.
> REFRAIN

—Henry Clay Work[1]

ANALOG LIVES AND DIGITAL LIVES

Here reflect with the group on the contrast between two kinds of clock or time-piece — those with second, minute, and hour hands that give a spatial sense of time, and those with only a digital readout — and their parallels with two "kinds" of time, chronos *and* kairos. *Which is a more accurate symbol or metaphor for one's experience of daily life? The segment concludes with the following prayer:*

Giver of Time

Surely I am not requested by You to do more than I can.
May I coordinate my hats (roles), purses (finances), pens (work), crayons (play), and computers (details).

May I enjoy each task, while it is occurring.
May I discern what to prune out of my life.
Forgive me for living for my children's bedtime, living for the end of the school semester, and living for the completion of a book.

Thank you for Your flexibility; may I accept it gracefully.

—Carolyn Stahl Bohler,
from *Prayer on Wings*[2]

"TEACH US TO NUMBER OUR DAYS, AND SO GET A HEART OF WISDOM"

Participants are invited to move around the room, studying the dates and calendar pages on the floor, and to pick up one sheet. With a partner or in triads, discuss what comes to your mind as holy about that particular date and day of the week in that particular month, either in a personal or communal sense.

HEARING THE WORD

Hebrews 4:1–3, 9–13

THE PRAYERS OF GOD'S PEOPLE

SINGING

"Be Still and Know," repeated from opening of service

BLESSING

NOTES

1. "My Grandfather's Clock" is in the public domain. A list of recorded sources may be found in *Rise Up Singing,* edited by Peter Blood-Patterson, copyright 1988 by Sing Out Corporation, P.O. Box 5253, Bethlehem, PA 18015; (215) 865-5366. Music may be found in the Burl Ives Songbook, *Songs for the Rotary Club, Singing Along with the World's Favorite Folk Songs, Folk Song Encyclopedia,* vol. 1, and *Best Loved Songs of the American People* — sources all listed in *Rise Up Singing.*

2. "On Ending the Day with More Things to Do" by Carolyn Stahl Bohler, reprinted from *Prayer on Wings,* © 1990 by LuraMedia, San Diego, CA 92121. Used with permission.

SUGGESTED ALTERNATE HYMNS

"Eternal God, Whose Power Upholds" (HB, LBW, MH, PH, TPH, WB)

"Give to the Winds Thy Fears" (HB, MH, PH, TPH, WB)

"If Thou but Suffer God to Guide Thee" (HB, HUCC, LBW, MH, PH, TPH, UMH, WB)

"Not So in Haste, My Heart" (HB, UMH)

"O [Our] God, Our Help in Ages Past" (HB, HUCC, LBW, PH, TPH, UMH)

15

THE POWER OF THE WORD

(Epiphany)

INTRODUCTION

Under the name of Holy Scripture, or the Word of God written, are now contained all the books of the Old and New Testaments. . . . All which are given by inspiration of God, to be the rule of faith and life.

—from "The Westminster Confession of Faith"

This service focuses on how we understand Scripture as the "Inspired Word of God." Everyone has an opinion to share on how they understand this book that is the foundation of our faith.

Let all interpretations be in accord with the "rule of love," the twofold commandment to love God and to love our neighbor. Augustine, whose thought summed up the theology of the early church and guided much of the early Middle Ages, articulated the rule of love. In contemporary language, his concern was something like this: If you hear someone interpreting Scripture in a way that does not elevate love for God or enhance love for neighbor, you should question the validity of that interpretation.

—from *The Presbyterian Understanding and Use of the Holy Scripture*[1]

PREPARATION

The room should be set up in a way that encourages discussion. The worship center is a table with a number of different translations or versions of the Bible. If it is possible in advance, participants should be invited to bring a Bible with them to be placed on the table as a visual reminder of how many ways the Bible is, and can be, interpreted. The following quotations may be printed on the bulletin cover, with participants encouraged to read these before worship begins:

The Bible is to be interpreted in the light of its witness to God's work of reconciliation in Christ. The Scriptures are nevertheless the words of [human beings], conditioned by the language, thought forms, and literary fashions of the places and times at which they were written. They reflect the views of life history, and the cosmos which were then current. . . . As God has spoken [the word] in diverse cultural situations, the church is confident that God will continue to speak through the Scriptures in a changing world and in every form of human culture. . . . God's word is spoken to the church today where the Scriptures are faithfully preached and attentively read in dependence on the illumination of the Holy Spirit and with readiness to receive their truth and direction.

—from the "Confession of 1967"

Years ago I heard a story about a seminary student who approached Paul Tillich following one of that great theologian's lectures. The student clutched a Bible which he thrust at Dr. Tillich while angrily asking, "Is this the inspired word of God or not?" Dr. Tillich smiled at the student and calmly replied, "It is if it grasps you rather than you grasping it."

—from *Eavesdropping on the Echoes*, Ted Loder[2]

❁

GATHERING WORDS (unison)

Your law, Yahweh, is perfect,
    it refreshes the soul.
Your rule is to be trusted,
    it gives wisdom to the simple.
Your precepts, Yahweh, are right,
    they gladden the heart.
Your command is clear,
    it gives light to the eyes.
Fear of you, Yahweh, is holy,
    abiding forever.
Your decrees are faithful,
    and all of them just.
They are more desirable than gold,
        than the purest of gold,
        and sweeter than honey are they,
        than honey oozing from the comb.
So in them your servant finds instruction;
    in keeping them is great reward.

> May the words of my mouth,
>   and the thoughts of my heart,
>   win favor in your sight, O Yahweh,
>   my Redeemer, my Rock!
>
>   —Psalm 19:7–11, 14

SONG

"O Word of God Incarnate," *The Presbyterian Hymnal*

A TIME OF CONFESSING
OUR SEPARATION FROM GOD (unison)

> To you, O God,
> we give up the burdens of this week,
> trusting your love and mercy.
> To you, O God,
> we surrender ourselves,
> trusting our risen Lord to lead us always
> in the way of peace,
> today, tomorrow, and forever.

Silence

Leader: Nothing can separate us from the love of God.

People: God's promise of love in Christ is for today, tomorrow, and forever. We believe we are forgiven, loved, and free. Amen.

SCRIPTURE READINGS

Nehemiah 8:1–4a, 5–6, 8–10
Luke 4:14–21

SOLO

"Jesus Was Sent," words and music by John Ylvisaker[3]

TIME OF REFLECTION AND DISCUSSION

Questions about the Bible

• What do we mean by the "inspired word of God?"

SONG

"Live into Hope," *The Presbyterian Hymnal*

SCATTERING

There is an ancient story of the Egyptian god Teuth, the inventor of the letters for writing. As Socrates tells it in Plato's dialogue "Phaedrus," Teuth brought his invention before the god Thamus, the king of Egypt, saying:

> This invention, O king, will make the Egyptians wiser and will improve their memories; for it is an elixir of memory and wisdom that I have discovered." But Thamus replied, "Most ingenious Teuth, one man has the ability to beget arts, but the ability to judge of their usefulness or harmfulness to their users belongs to another; and now you, who are the father of letters, have been led by your affection to ascribe to them a power the opposite of that which they really possess. For this invention will produce forgetfulness in the minds of those who learn to use it, because they will not practice their memory. Their trust in writing, produced by external characters which are no part of themselves, will discourage the use of their own memories within them. You have invented an elixir not of memory, but of reminding; and you offer your pupils the appearance of wisdom, not true wisdom, for they will read many things without instruction and will therefore seem to know many things, when they are for the most part ignorant and hard to get along with since they are not wise, but only appear wise" (*Phaedrus*, 274f).

—from *Experiments with Bible Study*[4]

❁

NOTES

1. Excerpt from *The Presbyterian Understanding and Use of Holy Scripture*, Office of the General Assembly Presbyterian Church, U.S.A. © 1992.

2. Excerpt from *Eavesdropping on the Echoes* by Ted Loder, © 1987 by LuraMedia, Inc., San Diego, CA 92121. Used with permission of publisher.

3. "Jesus Was Sent" by John Ylvisaker, from *Borning Cry*, vol. 1, published by Ylvisaker, Inc., Box 321, Waverly, IA 50677.

4. Excerpt from *Experiments with Bible Study* by Hans-Ruedi Weber, © 1981 WCC Publications, World Council of Churches, Geneva, Switzerland. Reproduced with permission.

SUGGESTED ALTERNATE HYMNS

"Break Thou the Bread of Life" (HB, LBW, MH, PH, TPH, UMH, WB)

"God's Word Is Perfect and Gives Life" (TPH)

"How Firm a Foundation" (HB, LBW, MH, PH, TPH, UMH, WB)

"Lamp of Our Feet" (HB, MH, PH)

"O God of Light" (HB, LBW, MH)

"The Rocks Would Shout If We Kept Still" (NHLC)

16

THE DISCIPLESHIP EMPLOYMENT OFFICE

(Epiphany)

INTRODUCTION

Divine invitations elicit strange responses from people. One of the authors of this volume, upon receiving a proposal of marriage from her future husband, was so taken aback that she betrayed all her feminist values by blurting out, "But you know I can't cook!" Similarly the prophet Isaiah, face to face with the awesome majesty of God, moaned "Woe is me! ... for I am a man of unclean lips...." And the weary, discouraged fishermen encountering Jesus on the lake of Gennesaret pulled up the catch of their lives but responded to this onrush of grace with Simon's words, "Go away from me, Lord, for I am a sinful man!" Nevertheless, consider: It is not necessarily God's intention that when we encounter the Holy we must see it as something we ourselves are *not*.

God flings out the invitation to discipleship meant for not-less-than-*everyone*: "Whom shall I send, and who will go for us?" But we are wont to respond like schoolchildren, with fear of the very thing we wanted most — whether being picked for the first team, auditioning successfully for the play, or being chosen by our beloved Source as bearers of the Spirit. Is it our fear of success? ("What are we gonna do with all these fish?" as Alan, our music director, put it.)

In the gospels, *overabundance* is a sign of the inbreaking of God's realm; and the fisher-disciples in their little boat offer a pointed challenge to modern people of faith who *also* tend to be afraid when a mission grows and succeeds. The final secret surprise, in this service as in the realm of God, is that *everybody's* qualifications are acceptable: Everyone who applies gets the job!

PREPARATION

The worship area is set up as much like an employment office as possible: with a large old wooden or metal desk in front, with rolling desk chair, separated from several rows of folding chairs by standards from which chains or velvet ropes are hung delineating the "line up" (as in a bank or airport

ticket counter). Two metal "in" baskets on the desktop hold stacks of Job
Application and Personal Recommendation forms: enough copies of the
former for every worshipper to receive one, and two of the latter for each.
(Sample forms are found at the end of this chapter.) Additional touches
may be added for "authenticity": outdated magazines in racks, a bare light
bulb overhead... anything that would evoke the atmosphere of a public
employment agency.

Other supplies needed for the service are gold notary seals *or* a large old
rubber stamp that says "HIRED" or "OK" or "APPROVED," with red ink
pad; and a supply of No. 2 lead pencils in various degrees of sharpness,
standing in a coffee can on the desk.

As worshippers enter, they are directed by an assistant at the door into
the line to pick up a Job Application from the front desk, and then to take
a seat.

❀

ENTERING THE EMPLOYMENT OFFICE

*A leader, acting throughout the service in the role of Personnel Officer, reads this
greeting prior to the singing of the hymn:*

Welcome! Anybody here nervous? Well, relax: God wouldn't have
called you for the interview if God didn't think you could do the job!
Now... Tell us what brought you here this morning.

SINGING

"He Called Me," words and music by Sr. Helen Marie Gitsdorf[1]

THE JOB DESCRIPTION

Isaiah 6:1–8
Luke 5:1–11

PRAYER OF CONFESSION:
FILLING OUT THE APPLICATION

*As the order of worship indicates, the filling out of the Job Application is the prayer
of confession: it might be noted that this is "where the rubber meets the road"!*

RESPONSE

"Lord, You Have Come to the Lakeshore," *The Presbyterian Hymnal*

GATHERING REFERENCES

After the Affirmation of Faith, Personal Recommendation forms are distributed, two apiece, to each worshipper to use in soliciting written "recommendations" from others. The process should be allowed ten to fifteen minutes, depending upon the size and speed of the group.

AFFIRMATION OF FAITH: 1 Corinthians 15:1–10

Personnel Officer:

"Now I would remind you, sisters and brothers, in what terms I preached to you the gospel, which you received, in which you stand, by which you are saved, if you hold it fast — unless you believed in vain."

All (singing): "This Is the Good News," *The Presbyterian Hymnal*

Personnel Officer:

"Then Christ appeared to James, then to the apostles."

All: "Last of all, as to one untimely born, Christ appeared also to me. For I am least of the apostles, unfit to be called an apostle, because I persecuted the church of God. But by the grace of God I am what I am, and God's grace toward me was not in vain. On the contrary, I worked harder than any of them, though it was not I, but the grace of God which is with me."

SUBMITTING APPLICATIONS AND REFERENCES

"Applicants" bring their applications and recommendation forms forward and deposit them again in the appropriate wire baskets. One or two assistants, briefed on the process in advance, sit down at the desk and begin to go through the papers, making a deliberate show of reading each and whispering to one another about them, sorting them into stacks, and loudly stamping them here and there. During this process, the Prayers of God's People go on, intercessions guided or led by the worship leader/"personnel officer."

THE HIRING: COMMISSIONS AND REJECTIONS

New members were being received on the day this service was held. We have left the questions for membership (from the Presbyterian tradition) in the liturgy to show a possible format for other churches. Whereas a pastor usually asks the questions of those seeking membership, on this day all were requested to join in reading them to emphasize the oneness of the whole body.

All read: Who is your Lord and Savior?

Do you trust in him?

Do you intend to be his disciple, to obey his word, and to show his love?

Will you be a faithful member of this congregation, giving of yourself in every way, and will you seek the fellowship of the church wherever you may be?

After the questions, the "personnel officer" announces that (s)he will distribute "commissions" and "rejections" one by one and that people should come forward when their names are called. Suspense should grow as the officer waits until the applicant has reached the front before announcing (in every case), "Application Approved!" and handing the stamped form to the person with a greeting such as "The peace of Christ be with you!" At a certain point it will begin to dawn upon worshippers that, contrary to their fears or expectations, all are being accepted for discipleship.

RESPONSE

"Here I Am, Lord," *The Presbyterian Hymnal*

BENEDICTION: The Welcoming of Fisherperson Recruits

FIRST ASSIGNMENT

The weekly sharing of Joys and Concerns is placed at the end of this service, emphasizing that disciples are sent out to care for the whole community. Here, with ample space under each heading for worshippers to write in notes for themselves, are listed the following headings:

- Those Who Are Ill:

- The Bereaved:

- Joys and Concerns:

- The Life of This Congregation:

❁

Along with the order of service outlined above, each worshipper receives a copy of the "Job Application" form, printed on a full page in large computer type, and two copies of the "Personal Recommendation" printed in large type. The text for these forms is included here; a copy-ready sample of each, in large type, is included in the Birthings and Blessings Resource Packet. For ordering information, see page 18.

JOB APPLICATION

Position: FISHERPERSON/EVANGELIST

Name _____

Age _____ Place of Birth _____

Education and/or previous training:

Previous Experience:

Strengths and Weaknesses:

What is your fisherperson philosophy? (Be brief.)

References (list two):

When available and/or willing to work? (circle all that apply)

full time   part-time   evenings   weekends

PERSONAL RECOMMENDATION

Position: FISHERPERSON/EVANGELIST

Recommendation written for (name of applicant):

How long have you known this person?

In what capacity?

PLEASE RATE THE APPLICANT ON HIS/HER QUALITIES
AS LISTED BELOW:

> 1 = Very poor
> 2 = Poor
> 3 = Good
> 4 = Excellent
> 5 = Outstanding

Dependability ____	Sense of Humor____
Clean Lips____	Good Judgment____
Eloquence____	Experience____
Efficiency____	Punctuality____
Thoroughness____	Creativity____
Compassion____	Attendance____
Cooperation____	Respect for Co-Workers____
Enthusiasm for Job____	Ability to Persuade____
Ability to Follow Instructions____	Adaptability to New or Changing Situations____

Additional Comments:

Signature of Reference Person _____

NOTES

1. "He Called Me" by Sr. Helen Marie Gitsdorf as found in *The Modern Liturgy,* Resource Publications, 7291 Coronado Dr., San Jose, CA 95129.

SUGGESTED ALTERNATE HYMNS

"Called as Partners in Christ's Service" (TPH)

"Christ of the Upward Way" (HB, TPH)

"How Clear Is Our Vocation, Lord" (TPH)

"Lord, You Have Come to the Lakeshore" (TPH, UMH)

"Take My Life" (HB, LBW, MH, PH, TPH, UMH)

"Take Up Your Cross, the Saviour Said" (HB, LBW, MH, TPH, UMH)

17

THE WINGS OF GOD

(Lent)

INTRODUCTION

This service focuses on the symbolism of wings — universally considered a symbol of spirituality. In some traditions birds are the very essence of the Deity. Wings are a metaphor for protection, shadow, shelter, the Temple itself in Jerusalem. The winged disk is an Egyptian symbol of the dawn of a new age, and the phoenix is a symbol of resurrection.

There is a contrast in feeling between eagle's wings and hen's wings; but both are important. Some people love to soar on eagles' wings. Others need the protection of hen's wings to be safe when they feel weak or vulnerable, or in need of nurture, a protected place. The Bible offers us both images: the protective cuddling wings of the hen and the soaring, empowering wings of the eagle. We need both depictions in order to know ourselves as loved and protected by God and fearlessly strengthened to soar.

PREPARATION

Chairs in two rows form a semicircle. The worship center, a round table, holds stuffed chickens and chicks.

Two large newsprint pads are needed. On one participants are asked to list words that describe "wings." On the other pad is a drawing of outstretched wings. In our service the following words were listed:

comfort	soaring	freedom
safety	thanksgiving	victory
beautiful	blue skies	manmade and natural
Pegasus	healing	liberation
dragonflies	powerful and gentle	angel
endurance	spirit	broken
encompassing	uplifting	frequent flyer miles
liberation	buffalo	jonathan livingston
	hot and spicy	

For this service the bulletin cover may be illustrated with chicken, eagle, and "healing" wings. The following passages may also be printed on the front:

O Jerusalem, Jerusalem, killing the prophets and stoning those who
are sent to you! How often would I have gathered your children together as a hen gathers her brood under her wings, and you would
not!

—Luke 13:34 RSV

But you also, Jesus, good Lord, are you not also Mother? Are you
not Mother, who are as a hen who gathers her own chicks under her
wings? Truly, Lord, you also are Mother. For that which others have
been in labor with and have borne, they have received from you.

—Anselm, eleventh century

But they who wait for the Lord shall renew their strength; they shall
mount up with wings like eagles, they shall run and not be weary, they
shall walk and not faint.

—Isaiah 40:31 RSV

For behold, the day comes, burning like an oven, when all the arrogant
and all evildoers will be stubble; the day that comes shall burn them
up, says the Lord of hosts, so that it will leave them neither root nor
branch. But for you who fear my name the sun of righteousness shall
rise with healing in its wings. You shall go forth leaping like calves
from the stall.

—Malachi 4:1–2

You have not as it were forsaken me, but your own selves, saith the
Lord. Thus says the Almighty Lord: Have I not prayed for you as
a father his sons, as a mother her daughters, and a nurse her young
babes, That ye would be my people, and I would be your God; that
ye would be my children, and I should be your father? I gathered you
together, as a hen gathers her chickens under her wings.

—2 Esdras 1:27–30 KJV

❁

GATHERING MUSIC (for listening)

SOLO

"Within Your Shelter, Loving God," *The Presbyterian Hymnal*

GATHERING WORDS

*The worship leader invites participants to fill in the newsprint with words that
describe "wings."*

SCRIPTURE READING

Luke 13:31–35

TIME OF DISCUSSION:
The Wings of God — Wings That Shelter, Wings That Soar

The worship leader reviews the action of the passage: Jesus moves from anger to lament. In these few verses we see Jesus make that transition. In verbalizing his anger, Jesus is moved to compassion. NOTE: The word "fox" in Hebrew means "destructive"; in Greek, it means "clever."

QUESTIONS FOR SMALL-GROUP DISCUSSION

- The wings of a chicken do not spread very far: under the wing we would be held close to the being of God. What aspect within yourself longs to be gathered under a protective wing?

- What is Jesus saying about God here?

SOLO

"Jerusalem," from *The Hymnal for Young Christians*[1]

LITANY

Leader: O God, you gather us;
            Your outspread wings gather us
            for protection, for comfort, for nurture.
            You hold us close, and we are at rest.

People: May we, too, gather in
            all those in need of protection and comfort,
            nurture and rest.
            May we spread our wings of caring.

Leader: O God, you invite us to return.
            Your wings offer a warm place,
            a home that is a place of love and compassion.

People: May we return to this home:
            a place we can be still,
            a place we feel your gentle touch.

Leader: O God, you comfort us.
            With your loving wings holding us close,
            we know ourselves to be loved by you.

People: May we in turn offer comfort,
            holding close those in need —
            those who hear for the first time:
            God is love.

Leader: O God, on your wings we soar.
            We live in your energy and spirit.
            You renew us;
            You encourage and strengthen.

People: May we in turn encourage and strengthen.
            May our strong wings uphold others
            that together we may soar unafraid.

                                              — Rosemary C. Mitchell

WINGS THAT SHELTER/WINGS THAT SOAR

The worship leader reviews the contrasts between the image of eagles' wings and hens' wings, leading to a time of prayer.

PRAYERS FOR OTHERS: Those in Need of God's Wings

The prayers are written on slips of paper shaped like feathers. Participants tape these to the wings drawn on newsprint: above the wings if they need to soar, below the wings if they need to be protected and cuddled.

THE PEACE

SONG

"Help Us Accept Each Other," *The Presbyterian Hymnal*

❁

NOTES

1. "Jerusalem" by Germaine Arr., Roget Nachtwey. © 1967 F.E.L. Church Publications, Ltd., 22 East Huron St. Chicago, IL 60611, as found in *Hymnal for Young Christians.*

SUGGESTED ALTERNATE HYMNS

"Christ, Whose Glory Fills the Skies" (HB, LBW, MH, PH, TPH, UMH, WB)

"Give to the Winds Thy Fears" (HB, MH, PH, TPH, UMH, WB)

"God of the Sparrow" (TPH, UMH)

"Immortal, Invisible, God Only Wise" (vv. 1–3: HB, HUCC, LBW, MH, PH, TPH, UMH, WB)

"Sing Praise to God Who Reigns Above" (HB, HUCC, LBW, MH, PH, TPH, UMH, WB)

"Eagles Spiraling Comply" (NHLC)

18

"JESUS, REMEMBER THEM..."

(A Good Friday Memorial)

Ellie Newell, a member of our congregation, responded to the special Lenten services of the year by writing a Trilogy for Lent on the themes of Ash Wednesday, Maundy Thursday, and Good Friday. In this third piece of the trilogy, she describes the service to follow:

Good Friday, 1992

The violence of the first "Good" Friday has been mirrored through the ages; it's reflected in this week's headlines and in the fine print of our lives.

News items form a litany:

- Woman accosted in parking lot
- Shots fired from car at random targets
- Stabbing ends neighbors' dispute
- Three families homeless, arsonists blamed
- Well-known businessman peddles cocaine to minors
- Baby hurled against a wall

But there's a subtler violence that never makes the news:

- Men and women deprived of jobs and meaningful work
- Children robbed of self-worth by their own parents
- Strength and wellness sapped by poor medical care
- Experience gained from age trampled under foot
- Creativity suffocated in the guise of education
- Ideas and initiative deadened by those in power

Do we still cry "Barabbas" and condone these violent acts? Do we stand alongside Pilate and refuse to get involved? Or do we come to Golgotha and like the thief seek mercy, then ask the wounded Christ to help us make each day "good"?

—Ellie Newell[1]

PREPARATION

While this Good Friday service may be adapted for use in a church sanctuary, a more flexible space — a fellowship hall or public gathering area (such as a city hall atrium) — is better suited to the movement of the liturgy.

Chairs are arranged in semicircular rows divided by a broad center aisle. This placement of seating creates a spacious area in front (preferably *not* a raised platform or stage) against a plain wall or wooden backdrop. The only focal point is a large, rough-hewn wooden cross (8 to 10 feet high) built of two-by-fours, its wood entirely covered with headlines jaggedly ripped from newspapers and taped around the beams. (The cross, which is freestanding, can be braced at its foot to a broad plywood base. A carpenter in the congregation built such a cross for us some years ago, and it has been brought out of church-cellar storage on numerous occasions for liturgical use.)

A large crown of thorns (fashioned from spiky branches by a member with horticultural skills, also a permanent piece of church "equipment") encircles the upright of the cross, tilted forward to hang supported by the crossbars. Draped from the "thorns" at three points on the crown (one from behind the crossbars) are three large "trickles of blood." These may be created from three strips (30" to 36" long and 4" wide) of bright red cotton fabric, each ripped into four or five narrower strips (one-half to two-thirds up from one end, and about one-quarter of the way from the other end) so that a solid length remains in the middle. It is by this intact section that the banners of "blood" hang from the crown of thorns. Ripping rather than scissoring the strips gives the fabric a slight jaggedness along the edges where threads are pulled, so that a powerfully realistic effect is created.

The only other props consist of one large, formal chair (which becomes Pilate's seat of judgment) such as might be borrowed from a church sanctuary or a formal living room; a small side table a few feet from the chair holding a basin of water and a towel; and baskets containing newspaper clippings. Prior to the service, leaders need to clip from recent newspapers headlines and articles having to do with incidents of "crucifixion" in the world. There should be enough items for as many worshippers as are anticipated at the service, although in a large group it may be more dramatic if only a few worshippers read aloud. Use a neon highlighter to mark the exact portions of the article that should be read: a brief identifying headline, and (if needed) a sentence or two from the body of the article to elaborate on the incident. "Family Killed in Crash; DWI Blamed" or "Researchers see number of children orphaned by AIDS rising steadily" are examples of the concerns that might be used. Planners should not be afraid to include ironic or bittersweet, unexpected items: all sections of the newspaper should be searched, in addition to the front page.

The script (printed here in the body of the service) is given only to the Narrator, Pilate, and Jesus; and, while they refer to the script as they speak, the dramatization should be well rehearsed in advance for voice level, inflection, and minimal "choreography" for the two main characters. The printed order of worship in the hands of participants will be a simple two- or three-page bulletin with the readings noted only by their title and chapter/verse references, so that worshippers have the full impact of seeing and hearing the action.

A worship leader wearing either street clothes or liturgical garb may act as Narrator. We found it extremely effective to cast a young adult male as a Jesus with avant-garde haircut, wearing casual slacks and shirt, and an older, reserved, "executive" type in conservative business suit as Pontius Pilate. Different nuances could be created by selecting women instead of men for these parts.

Effective lighting is muted but stark — just bright enough for people to read — with stationary spotlights on the cross and staging area. Participants in our service were struck by the unexpected and dramatic shadows cast by the cross against the background wall, to which we had affixed a large backdrop of white butcher paper. On it had been sketched simple line drawings of human figures on two hillside crosses, framing the wooden cross. Samples of this minimalist style can be found in Annie Valottin's sketches throughout *The Good News Bible* (American Bible Society).

CALL TO WORSHIP: Isaiah 53:1, 3–4

Leader: Who has believed what we have heard?
And to whom has the arm of God been revealed?
He was despised and rejected by everyone,
a man of sorrows, and acquainted with grief.

People: Surely he has borne our griefs and carried our sorrows,
yet we esteemed him stricken,
smitten by God, and afflicted.

PRAYER (unison)

Christ our victim,
whose beauty was disfigured
and whose body was torn upon the cross;
open wide your arms
to embrace our tortured world,

that we may not turn away our eyes,
but abandon ourselves to your mercy.
Amen.

—Janet Morley, *All Desires Known*

HYMN

"What Wondrous Love Is This?" *The Presbyterian Hymnal*

FIRST READING: The Trial (John 18:28–19:16)[2]

Narrator stands to one side of the front "staging" area to read. As reading begins, Jesus walks up the center aisle from the back, and turns to face the "crowd." Pilate enters from the side, standing slightly behind Jesus and to one side of him.

Narrator: They then led Jesus from the house of Caiaphas to the Praetorium. It was now morning. They did not go into the Praetorium themselves or they would be defiled and unable to eat the passover. So Pilate came outside to them and said,

Pilate: What charge do you bring against this man?

Narrator: They replied, "If he were not a criminal, we should not be handing him over to you."

Pilate: Take him yourselves, and try him by your own Law.

Narrator: The Jews answered, "We are not allowed to put a man to death." This was to fulfil the words Jesus had spoken indicating the way he was going to die. [*Pilate turns and takes a few steps back, turns again to face the congregation, and Jesus turns to face Pilate (his back to congregation).*] So Pilate went back into the Praetorium and called Jesus to him, and asked,

Pilate: Are you the king of the Jews?

Jesus: Do you ask this of your own accord, or have others spoken to you about me?

Pilate: Am I a Jew? It is your own people and the chief priests who have handed you over to me: what have you done?

Jesus: Mine is not a kingdom of this world; if my kingdom were of this world, my men would have fought to prevent me being surrendered to the Jews. But my kingdom is not of this kind.

Pilate: So you are a king then?

Jesus: It is you who say it. Yes, I am a king. I was born for this, I
            came into the world for this; to bear witness to the truth,
            and all who are on the side of truth listen to my voice.

Pilate: Truth? What is that? [*These words are followed by a dramatic
            pause.*]

Narrator: And with that he went out again to the Jews and said, [*As
            Pilate speaks, Jesus turns to face the crowd.*]

Pilate: I find no case against him. But according to a custom of
            yours I should release one prisoner at the Passover; would
            you like me, then, to release the king of the Jews?

Narrator: At this they shouted:

*One person rises from the midst of the congregation to read all lines where "Voice"
is indicated. S/he may move into the center aisle, moving in and out of the pew
and up and down the aisle, performing the lines with a fierce and agitated voice.*

Voice: Not this man, but Barabbas.

Narrator: Barabbas was a brigand. Pilate then had Jesus taken away
            and scourged; [*Jesus moves back up the aisle, to stand three-
            fourths of the way toward the back of the worship space*] and
            after this, the soldiers twisted some thorns into a crown
            and put it on his head, and dressed him in a purple robe.
            They kept coming up to him and saying,

*The performer of the "voice" moves to where Jesus is standing and shouts his/her
lines, angrily, close to Jesus' face.*

Voice: Hail, king of the Jews!

Narrator: And they slapped him in the face. Pilate came outside
            again [*Pilate moves to a spot just in front of the first row of
            worshippers.*] and said to them,

Pilate: Look, I am going to bring him out to you to let you see
            that I find no case.

Narrator: Jesus then came out [*Jesus moves deliberately up the aisle
            again, toward Pilate.*] wearing the crown of thorns and
            the purple robe. Pilate said,

Pilate: Here is the man.

Narrator: When they saw him the chief priests and the guards
            shouted,

Voice: Crucify him! Crucify him!

Pilate: Take him yourselves and crucify him: I can find no case
            against him.

Voice: We have a Law, and according to the Law he ought to die, because he has claimed to be the son of God.

Narrator: When Pilate heard them say this his fears increased. Re-entering the Praetorium, [*Pilate moves back into the staging area, to stand in front of the chair.*] he said to Jesus,

Pilate: Where do you come from?

Narrator: But Jesus made no answer.

Pilate: Are you refusing to speak to me? Surely you know I have power to release you and I have power to crucify you.

Jesus: You would have no power over me if it had not been given you from above; that is why the one who handed me over to you has the greater guilt.

Narrator: From that moment Pilate was anxious to set him free, but the Jews shouted,

Voice: If you set him free you are no friend of Caesar's; anyone who makes himself king is defying Caesar.

Narrator: Hearing these words, Pilate had Jesus brought out, and seated himself on the chair of judgment [*Pilate seats himself heavily in the large chair.*] at a place called the Pavement, in Hebrew Gabbatha. It was Passover Preparation Day, about the sixth hour. Pilate said to the Jews,

Pilate: Here is your king.

Voice: Take him away, take him away. Crucify him!

Pilate: Do you want me to crucify your king?

Narrator: The chief priests answered, We have no king except Caesar. So in the end Pilate handed him over to them, to be crucified.

Jesus walks slowly to the cross and stands facing it, his back to worshippers; Pilate remains seated, and Jesus remains standing in place, throughout the following prayers and hymn.

PRAYERS OF THE PEOPLE

Here should be printed the melody lines as well as the words of the traditional minor-key "Lord, have mercy upon us" (WB, TPH), divided in segments as follows:

I. Lord, have mercy upon us.

II. Christ, have mercy upon us.

III. Lord, have mercy upon us.

Worshippers are asked to read their highlighted headlines aloud, in turn, up and down the rows. After every three or four readings — depending upon number of participants — one line of the "Lord, have mercy" response is sung. This reading/singing cycles over and over, in an attitude of prayer, until all have read.

SILENCE

HYMN

"He Never Said a Mumbalin' Word," *The Presbyterian Hymnal*

SECOND READING: The Drama of the End (John 19:17–30)

Narrator: They then took charge of Jesus, and carrying his own cross he went out of the city to the place of the skull, or, as it was called in Hebrew, Golgotha, where they crucified him with two others, one on either side with Jesus in the middle. *[Jesus turns in place in front of the cross to face worshippers, face tilted upward to gaze at the ceiling, neck exposed.]* Pilate wrote out a notice and had it fixed to the cross; it ran: "Jesus the Nazarene, King of the Jews." This notice was read by many of the Jews, because the place where Jesus was crucified was not far from the city, and the writing was in Hebrew, Latin, and Greek. So the Jewish chief priests said to Pilate, "You should not write 'King of the Jews,' but 'This man said: I am King of the Jews.'

Pilate: What I have written, I have written. *[Pilate rises from his seat and walks silently down the aisle to disappear behind the congregation.]*

Narrator: When the soldiers had finished crucifying Jesus they took his clothing and divided it into four shares, one for each soldier. His undergarment was seamless, woven in one piece from neck to hem; so they said to one another, "Instead of tearing it, let's throw dice to decide who is to have it." In this way the words of Scripture were fulfilled:

They shared out my clothing among them.
They cast lots for my clothes.

This is exactly what the soldiers did.

Near the cross of Jesus stood his mother and his mother's sister, Mary the wife of Clopas, and Mary of Magdala. Seeing his mother and the disciple he loved standing near her, Jesus said to his mother, [*Jesus fixes his gaze down toward the congregation before saying the next lines, addressing one side with "This is your son" and the other side with "This is your mother."*]

Jesus: Woman, this is your son.

Narrator: Then to the disciple he said,

Jesus: This is your mother.

Narrator: And from that moment the disciple made a place for her in his home.

After this, Jesus knew that everything had now been completed, and to fulfil the Scripture perfectly he said:

Jesus: I am thirsty.

Narrator: A jar full of vinegar stood there, so putting a sponge soaked in vinegar on a hyssop stick they held it up to his mouth. After Jesus had taken the vinegar he said,

Jesus: It is accomplished.

Narrator: And bowing his head he gave up the spirit.

Still standing directly in front of the cross, Jesus lets his head drop limply forward. If the cross has been spotlighted until now, the light should be cut or dimmed as the solo begins. On the last lines of the song, Jesus silently leaves the staging area through the shadows, out a side exit if possible.

SOLO

"Hammering," from *American Negro Songs and Spirituals*[3]

PRAYER

Holy one,
shock and save me with the terrible goodness of this Friday,
and drive me deep into my longing for your kingdom
until I seek it first —
    yet not first for myself,
but for the hungry
    and the sick
        and the poor of your children,
for prisoners of conscience around the world,
for those I have wasted

with my racism
   and sexism
      and nationalism
         and religionism,
for those around this mother earth and in *this* city
who, this Friday, know far more of terror than of goodness.

Jesus, remember them
   remember me
   remember us
when you come into your realm.

—Ted Loder, *Guerillas of Grace* (adapted)[4]

THIRD READING: The Burial (John 19:31–34, 38–42)

Narrator: It was Preparation Day, and to prevent the bodies remaining on the cross during the sabbath — since that sabbath was a day of special solemnity — the Jews asked Pilate to have the legs broken and the bodies taken away. Consequently the soldiers came and broke the legs of the first man who had been crucified with him and then of the other. When they came to Jesus, they found that he was already dead, and so instead of breaking his legs one of the soldiers pierced his side with a lance; and immediately there came out blood and water.

After this, Joseph of Arimathaea, who was a disciple of Jesus — though a secret one because he was afraid of the Jews — asked Pilate to let him remove the body of Jesus. Pilate gave permission, so they came and took it away. Nicodemus came as well — the same one who had first come to Jesus at night-time — and he brought a mixture of myrrh and aloes, weighing about a hundred pounds. They took the body of Jesus and wrapped it with the spices in linen cloths, following the Jewish burial custom. At the place where he had been crucified there was a garden, and in the garden a new tomb in which no one had yet been buried. Since it was the Jewish Day of Preparation and the tomb was near at hand, they laid Jesus there.

SINGING

"Jesus, Remember Me," *The Presbyterian Hymnal*

BENEDICTION

The people leave in silence

❀

NOTES

1. "Good Friday, 1992" by Ellie Newell, Fairport, N.Y. Used with permission of author.

2. The Scripture selections from the Gospel of John are drawn from the Jerusalem Bible, © 1966 Doubleday & Co., Inc.

3. "Hammering," ed. John W. Work, © 1940 John W. Work, included in *Faith, Folk, and Clarity*, Galaxy Music Corporation, 2121 Broadway, New York, NY 10023.

4. The Prayer is by Ted Loder from *Guerrillas of Grace*, © 1984 by LuraMedia, Inc., San Diego, CA 92121. Used by permission of publisher.

SUGGESTED ALTERNATE HYMNS

"How Long, O Lord, How Long?" (NHLC)

"O Sacred Head Now Wounded" (HB, HUCC, LBW, MH, PH, TPH, UMH, WB)

"O Young and Fearless Prophet" (MH, UMH vv. 1, 2, 4, 5)

"Today We Are All Called to Be Disciples" (TPH, UMH)

"We Meet You, O Christ" (TPH, UMH)

"Were You There" (HB, HUCC, LBW, MH, PH, TPH, UMH)

"When I Survey" (HB, HUCC, LBW, MH, PH, TPH, UMH, WB)

19

HANDS

(First Sunday after Easter)

INTRODUCTION

"Unless I see in [Jesus'] hands the print of the nails, and place my finger in the mark of the nails, and place my hand in his side, *I will not believe.*" By touching, Thomas knew, the other is lifted from the abstract and made a *real person.* Cynicism leapt instantaneously to faith once Thomas saw, felt, and was able to touch the risen Christ.

Thomas instinctively knew something that many people of faith choose to discount: that faith is made real, and we are made real to one another, not by the abstractions of our theology but by the presence of God mediated through the physical. As Presbyterian poet/hymnwriter Dr. Thomas Troeger has written,

> These things did Thomas count as real:
> The warmth of blood, the chill of steel,
> The grain of wood, the heft of stone,
> The last frail twitch of flesh and bone...[1]

On the Sunday after Easter, like Jesus, "whose raw, imprinted palms reached out / And beckoned Thomas from his doubt..." we too can beckon one another into a more solid experience of faith by extending our hands.

PREPARATION

On the front of the order of worship for this day, a hand print is superimposed with the words of Thomas "Unless I see in his hands...." Underneath the image are printed the words of the hymn "These Things Did Thomas Count as Real" — a hymn that is sung by the community or by a soloist within the service.

To prepare the worship setting, two large cardboard refrigerator boxes procured from an appliance store are rebuilt: The back side is cut away, leaving a three-sided "booth," and the back half of the top is also trimmed off (leaving a half-roof to prevent a person sitting inside from seeing out the front). A round hole approximately 6″ in diameter is cut in the center front, and crepe paper streamers are taped to hang down over the hole from inside so that a human hand can be placed through the hole but its owner is not visible from within. A chair or low stool is placed inside each three-walled booth, and another in front: an arrangement vaguely resembling a confessional.

Other supplies needed for the service are scissors (a pair for every four or five worshippers), pencils or felt markers, and colored construction paper.

PRELUDE

"Reach Out and Touch Somebody's Hand," Ashford and Simpson[2]

THE CALL TO GATHER

1 John 1:1–4

SINGING

"Spirit of New Life"[3]

OUR BODILY CONFESSION (antiphonally)

Worshippers repeat both words and gestures antiphonally after the leader. Only the first line — "Lord, here are our hands" — is actually printed in the order of worship.

"Lord, here are our hands . . . "
  [*hands outstretched*]

Put in deep pockets to keep them safe,
  [*hands thrust into pockets*]

Held behind our backs to keep them hidden from you,
  [*hands placed behind back*]

Placed over our eyes to blind ourselves to the needs of others,
  [*hands held over eyes*]

Buried within sand where they are immobilized and useless,
  [*fingers entwined and clenched, hands thrust downward toward floor*]

Patting ourselves on the back to take credit for all we are and do,
  [*one hand exaggeratedly patting one's own back*]

Grabbing for the material things of life,
  [*both hands grabbing and clawing at imaginary treasures in the air*]

Forever pushing you away.
  [*both hands flattened, fingers splayed, one in front of the other with palms out, pushing upward as if to hold God at bay*]

AND OUR BODILY ASSURANCE

Again, participants repeat after leader, arms extended and palms up. Only the first line need be printed in the order of worship:

> Lord, here are your hands:
> Tireless and always there for us.
> Beckoning us to come closer.
> Holding us secure.
> Lifting us up when we are down.
> Opening new doors for us.
> Revealing special gifts you have given us.
> Showing the way to eternal life.
> Touching us with overwhelming love.
> We are never the same again.
>
> —from "Hand in Hand: A Litany,"
> by Sue Downing[4]

HEARING THE GOSPEL: John 20:19–31

> *Reader:*   But Thomas said to them,
>
> *All:*   "Unless I see in Jesus' hands the print of the nails, and place my finger in the mark of the nails, and place my hand in Jesus' side, *I will not believe.*"

CONTEMPLATING THE GOSPEL

"These Things Did Thomas Count as Real," Thomas Troeger and Carol Doran

Either sung as a solo, or sung thoughtfully by the entire community.

EXPERIENCING THE GOSPEL

The leader invites two worshippers to enter the "booths" and be seated inside. Two others are silently chosen to take their places on chairs in front of the booths, putting one hand through the covered opening. Those inside the booths are asked to examine the hand: first by feel and then, opening their eyes, by sight (here, refer the group to 1 John 1:1). They are asked to describe the person, aloud, from the characteristics of the hand; and finally, to guess each identity. The two "subjects" then go to a supply table to trace their hands onto construction paper, cut them out, and write on them characteristics accurately cited by the "palm reader" and those owned by the subjects themselves — such as "working . . . sensitive . . . articulate . . . playing the piano." Participants rotate until everyone in the group has had palms "read" and/or read another's hand.

SINGING

"O Sons and Daughters, Let us Sing!" using the stanzas for the Second
Sunday of Easter

THE PRAYERS OF GOD'S PEOPLE

Bidding prayers suggested by a leader and prayed silently by participants:

I invite you to envision the following hands in your mind's eye and sense
in your heart, in each case, that these are the hands of Christ as well:

- wounded hands
- starving, bony hands
- hands of a friend beloved by you
- hands of an enemy: take and hold *that* hand in your own.

*The silent prayers are followed by the following closing litany, printed in the order
of worship:*

All:	Lord, we place our hands in yours.
Men:	Take them to use as you will.
Women:	No other hands can touch in quite the same way as ours.
All:	Lord, hand in hand with you, we are:
Men:	Reaching out in love to others,
Women:	inviting all to experience the abundant life,
All:	receiving much more than we give.

Lord, alone our hands are weak, but together with yours
they are strong. Amen.

—Sue Downing

SINGING

"Peace I Leave with You"[5]

BLESSING...

Participants exchange their cut-out hands with another with words of benediction.

POSTLUDE

"Reach Out and Touch..."

❀

NOTES

1. The words to "These Things Did Thomas Count as Real" from *New Hymns for the Lectionary — To Glorify the Maker's Name.* Music by Carol Doran, words by Thomas H. Troeger. New York: Oxford University Press, © 1986.

2. "Reach Out and Touch" by Ashford & Simpson, published by C.T.P./Belwin, 15800 N.W. 48th Ave., Miami, FL 33014.

3. "Spirit of New Life," © 1961 The Benedictine Foundation of the State of Vermont, Inc., Weston, VT 05161.

4. Assurance of Pardon and Litany from "Hand in Hand: A Litany" by Sue Downing, as found in *alive now* March/April 1991.

5. "Peace," © 1971 The Benedictine Foundation.

SUGGESTED ALTERNATE HYMNS

"Come, Ye Faithful, Raise the Strain" (HB, LBW, MH, PH, TPH, UMH, WB)

"Lord, Speak to Me" (HB, LBW, MH, PH, TPH, UMH)

"Many and Great, O God" (MH, TPH, UMH)

"Take My Life, and Let It Be" (HB, LBW, MH, PH, TPH, UMH)

"We Need Each Other's Voice to Sing" (NHLC)

"Your Hand, O Lord, in Days of Old" (LBW)

20

ORDINARY TIME— ORDINARY LIVES

(Ordinary Time)

INTRODUCTION

It is a difficult parable in two "acts" that Jesus tells to the Pharisees (and all who have ears to hear!). The parable may be understood as likening God to a king who sends out an invitation to a son's wedding feast. Not only are the invitations refused, however, but the messengers themselves are killed. Why would a person turn down such an invitation?

Act II begins in an exciting way: with a *new* invitation issued to people from the streets, "both good and bad." This time the focus is on those who *do* accept the invitation but have no idea what they have accepted. It is a tale about conversion and integrity: that accepting God's invitation means we live our lives in a different way. The message indeed is for us all, but at some point more will be asked of us — more than saying "Yes, Lord" or "I do believe." We must put on the clothing of discipleship; we must act on what we say we profess.

PREPARATION

This service does not require elaborate preparation, but it is helpful to recruit readers ahead of time. The room should be arranged to allow for small-group discussion.

❁

ORDINARY DISAPPOINTMENTS: Deuteronomy 34:1–12

Voice 1:   And Moses went up from the plains of Moab to Mt. Nebo, to the top of Pisgah, which is opposite Jericho. And God showed Moses all the land, Gilead as far as Dan, all Naphtali, the land of Ephraim and Manasseh, all the land of Judah as far as the Western Sea, the Negeb, and the Plain, that is, the valley of Jericho the city of palm trees, as far as Zoar. And God said to Moses:

All: This is the land of which I swore to Abraham, to Isaac, and to Jacob, "I will give it to your descendants." I have let you see it with your eyes, but you shall not go over there.

Voice 2:   So Moses the servant of God died there in the land of Moab, according to the word of God, and God buried Moses in the valley in the land of Moab; but no one knows the place of Moses' burial to this day. Moses was a hundred and twenty years old when he died; his eye was not dim, nor his natural force abated.

All: And the people of Israel wept for Moses in the plains of Moab thirty days; then the days of weeping and mourning for Moses were ended.

Voice 1:   And since then, there has not arisen a prophet in Israel like Moses, whom God knew face to face,

Voice 2:   none like Moses for all the signs and the wonders which God sent him to do in the land of Egypt, to Pharaoh and to all his servants and to all his land,

Voice 3:   and for all the mighty power and all the great and terrible deeds which Moses wrought in the sight of all Israel.

UNISON PRAYER

O God, we have had our own disappointments.
Like Moses, you have given us a glimpse of how life might be.
We question if we have the strength or the life in us to go forward,
    to move toward the dream of new life.
We know we are working as hard as we can.
We want to be appreciated like Moses.
We want God to appreciate us.
We want our family and friends to appreciate us.
We need assurance that you and others care about us.
We are sometimes more human than we can handle.
Forgive us and give us strength and courage for the living of our days.

—Rosemary C. Mitchell

EXTRA-ORDINARY GRACE FROM GOD AND FROM EACH OTHER

Leader: Friends, God cares about us more than our hearts and minds can imagine. We need to care about each other and take the time to say that to one another. We are forgiven and given the power of Christ's Spirit to live with courage and strength.

People: We sometimes feel like strangers, to God and to each other. We remember we are the friends of Christ, called to be friends for each other.

Leader: As friends, may the peace of Christ be with each of you.

People: And also with you.

SONG

"O God, Above the Drifting Years," *The Presbyterian Hymnal*

ACT I: AN ORDINARY INVITATION

SCRIPTURE READING

Matthew 22:1–10

READING

Excuses

"Why not?" that was the first thing he said. He had never seen me before. I hadn't said a word. "Why not?" I knew he had me.

I brought up excuses: "My wife... the people I have to work with... not enough time... I guess it's my temperament...." There was a sword hanging on the wall. He took it and gave it to me. "Here, with this sword, you can cut through any barriers." I took it and slipped away without saying a word.

Back in my room in the guesthouse I sat down and kept looking at that sword. I knew that what he said was true. But the next day I returned his sword. How can I live without my excuses?

—from *Tales of a Magic Monastery,*
Theophane the Monk[1]

SONG

"The Wedding Banquet," The Medical Mission Sisters[2]

CONVERSATION: THE EXTRA-ORDINARY RESPONSES

Discussion in small groups and then sharing with entire group:

• Why would folks turn down an invitation to a party?

ACT II: AN ORDINARY GUEST

SCRIPTURE READING

Matthew 22:11–14

CONVERSATION: AN EXTRA-ORDINARY HOST

- Why did the king throw out the wedding guest?
- What does this passage say about God?
- What does this passage say about us?

SONG

"Peace," Gregory Norbet, O.S.B.[3]

PRAYERS OF THE PEOPLE

LORD'S PRAYER

OFFERING

CLOSING (unison)

> Now, as friends:
> May all that is true,
> all that is noble,
> all that is just and right,
> all that is lovable and gracious,
> whatever is excellent and admirable,
> fill our thoughts and our hearts.
>
> —Philippians 4:8

❋

NOTES

1. "Excuses," from *Tales of a Magic Monastery* by Theophane the Monk, © 1988 by Crossroad Publishing Co., 370 Lexington Ave., New York, NY 10017.

2. "The Wedding Banquet" by Medical Mission Sisters, published by Vanguard Music Corp., Philadelphia, © 1965.

3. "Peace" by Gregory Norbet, O.S.B., Weston Priory Productions, Weston, VT 05161.

SUGGESTED ALTERNATE HYMNS

"Christ Is Made the Sure Foundation" (HB, HUCC, LBW, MH, PH, TPH, UMH, WB)

"God's Law is Perfect and Gives Life" (TPH)

"In Christ There Is No East or West" (HB, HUCC, vv. 1, 2, 4; LBW, MH, PH, vv. 1, 2, 4; TPH, UMH, WB)

"The Church's One Foundation" (HB, HUCC, LBW, MH, PH, TPH, UMH, WB)

21

FROM RAGE TO RECONCILIATION

(Ordinary Time)

INTRODUCTION

In early May 1992, a jury in California acquitted four white police officers of the beating of a black man named Rodney King. This decision sparked riots in Los Angeles and in other metropolitan areas, including our own city. This service was created for the following Sunday in order to allow people geographically removed from the event time for reflection on their feelings and dialogue about implications for our life together in society.

PREPARATION

Chairs are arranged in a half circle, with seven empty chairs set at the open end in a straight row. Seven members of the congregation are invited in advance to "play a character" in the service. Following the song "We Are Called to Follow Jesus," the worship leader introduces each character as a "visitor" to worship and welcomes them.

❈

GATHERING WORDS (unison)

Lead us from death to life,
from falsehood to truth.
Lead us from despair to hope,
from fear to trust.
Let peace fill our hearts,
our world, our universe.
Let us dream together,
pray together,
work together,
to build one world
of peace and justice for all.

—Anonymous, from
Prayers and Poems–Songs and Stories[1]

SONG

"God Will Guide Me"[2]

PRAYER OF AFFIRMATION (unison)

I am no longer afraid of death,
I know well
its dark and cold corridors
leading to life.

I am afraid rather of that life
which does not come out of death
which cramps our hands
and retards our march.

I am afraid of my fear
and even more of the fear of others,
who do not know where they are going,
who continue clinging
to what they consider to be life
which we know to be death!

I live each day to kill death;
I die each day to beget life,
and in this dying unto death,
I die a thousand times and
am reborn another thousand
through that love
from my People,
which nourishes hope!

—Julia Esquivel
from *Threatened with Resurrection*[3]

HEARING GOD'S VOICE THROUGH SCRIPTURE

Isaiah 40

SOLO

"We Are Called to Follow Jesus," words and music by Jim Strathdee[4]

HEARING THE VOICES OF HUMANITY

The worship leader introduces each "character," and they are invited to take a seat up front. Each person reads her/his part and then stays in character for the dialogue. The lines for each character were pieced together from newspaper and magazine clippings from the week of the verdict.

MILES TAYLOR, Los Angeles

My name is Miles Taylor. I am forty-nine years old and black. Since 1965 I have lived in south Los Angeles, in the neighborhood where the riots were last week. I remember the date because that was the year of the Watts riots when thirty-four people died. A traffic arrest started that riot, too. When the reporter spoke with me, I had to keep wiping ashes from my eyes. The ashes were from the flames of my friend's furniture store. A lot of it doesn't make sense. We've been through this before. They destroy their own community and then what do they do? I saw Betty Young crying near the supermarket down the street. She said to me, "This ain't going to help. All this burning. It's sad. The woman who runs the market, she's so sweet. She always cashed my disability check."

JACK GOLDSTEIN, Rochester, New York

My name is Jack Goldstein. I live in Rochester, New York. I have owned Goldstein's Clothing Market on Main Street for thirty years. I don't regret the risk I took on Friday, May 1. I saw a crowd turn over a police van in front of my shop and then smash the windows of the Busy Bee restaurant next door. So one of the guys who works for me and I grabbed our 12-gauge shotguns and stood in the doorway. I had another one of my guys grab a baseball bat. Then we watched what went on outside. We figured if they saw our weapons they would back off. This is a very, very pathetic thing for a man to have to do, but that's the way it goes. It's called fend for your life. I didn't feel that the police could defend me or my property adequately and watching what was going on at Midtown made us all very nervous. The police said we should close, but I decided not too. The display of weapons was absolutely necessary for the protection of my staff and myself.

MARY WELCH, Rochester, New York

My name is Mary Welch. I am seventeen years old and I live in Rochester, New York, where I am a student at Marshall High School. I didn't like the verdict. I'm mad about that, but I wouldn't be in a riot. It didn't make sense. They went after innocent people, and that wasn't right. I didn't think it was right. I think it is really bad what went on here in Rochester. I didn't like what was going on because they're making it harder on themselves in the movement. The only thing it accomplishes is people going to jail or being subject to a curfew. I think many people who participated in Rochester's trouble simply wanted to have Rochester noted for joining the unrest taking place in other cities. They just want to be like the rest. My friend here, Mysta Tein, agrees with me. He thinks they just want to be like L.A. They wanted to do the things L.A. was doing. So they can get a name. So they can get on TV.

CHRISTOPHER MORGAN, *Ventura Country, California*

My name is Christopher Morgan, and I was one of the jurors in the Rodney King beating trial. I defend the verdict we came to but I feel a little responsible for all the rioting. My first reaction was, "Oh, my God, I've been part of something that is completely out of control." You have to feel some sense of responsibility for the rioting. I am absolutely sure we made the right decision. It's impossible for others to judge without having sat through the trial. I was very conscious of this and how it would affect people. I'm not a prejudiced person. Everybody is so shocked by the verdict, but they weren't there. They didn't go through what we had to go through. The hate mail and threatening telephone calls are really terrible.

STEVE GATES, *Los Angeles*

My name is Steve Gates, and I am a Los Angeles police captain in charge of South Central L.A. Command Post. We are overwhelmed. When you see on television looters right in front of police officers, we have a horrible situation. The violence has been mainly in a seven-by-fifteen-mile area, but it spread to other neighborhoods. I have told the officers that their first priority is to protect themselves and fire fighters, two of whom were wounded by gunfire. One fire fighter said he would feel more secure if we would give him a rifle. Three of my officers have already been killed by rioters.

REGINALD DENNY, *Los Angeles*

My name is Reginald Denny. I was driving my eighteen-wheeler truck on my regular run through south central Los Angeles on Friday. What I remember is being pulled from the cab of my truck by a group of blacks and they started beating me. The television cameras showed that one person yanked open the door and pulled me from the cab. Two others beat my head and kicked me, then someone hit me with a fire extinguisher. I was lying on the street bleeding and I sensed that people were throwing things at me as I came in and out of consciousness. I crawled back to my truck inch by inch. I know now that five black strangers came to my rescue. They brought me unconscious to the hospital. The doctor said, "One more minute and he would have been dead."

VIRGINIA LOYA, *Ventura County, California*

My name is Virginia Loya. I was one of the jurors in the Rodney King beating trial and the only Hispanic. I prayed and fasted during the deliberations and I asked God to help me get out of this. The other jurors' eyes weren't open and I said to God, "If you could give me one more person on my side I would know." On the seventh and last day of the deliberations one other juror joined me and the other two who wanted to convict officer Laurence Powell on an assault charge. I was mocked by other jurors when I kept asking to see the videotape replayed. They would say, "Oh, Virginia wants to see the tape again." Others said they had seen it enough. The pressure was enormous to go along and I found myself in tears often. This was my first time as a member of a jury, and I always thought it was an honor. Now I don't know.

QUESTION FOR DISCUSSION

- What voice do you long to hear?

READING: The Response of Rodney King

People, I just want to say can we all get along? Can we stop making it horrible for the older people and the kids? . . . We'll get our justice. They've won their battle but they haven't won the war. We'll get our day in court.

PRAYERS OF THE PEOPLE

SONG

"Here I Am," *The Presbyterian Hymnal*

THE PEACE AND THE SCATTERING OF GOD'S PEOPLE INTO THE WORLD

❁

NOTES

1. The Call to Worship ("Gathering Words") is an anonymous prayer reproduced from *Ecumenical Decade 1988–1998, Churches in Solidarity with Women: Prayers & Poems–Songs & Stories*, WCC Publications, World Council of Churches, Geneva, Switzerland, 1988.

2. "God Will Guide Me," text: © 1989, John Ylvisaker; tune: public domain.

3. The Prayer of Affirmation is a poem entitled "I Am Not Afraid of Death" by Julia Esquivel, from *Threatened with Resurrection,* © 1982 by The Brethren Press, Elgin, IL 60120.

4. "We Are Called to Follow Jesus" by Jim Strathdee, © 1978 Desert Flower Music. As found in *Borning Cry,* vol. 2, published by John Ylvisaker, Box 321, Waverly, IA 50677.

SUGGESTED ALTERNATE HYMNS

"Forgive Our Sins as We Forgive" (LBW, TPH, UMH)

"Help Us Accept Each Other" (TPH, UMH)

"How Long, O Lord, How Long" (NHLC)

"Lift Every Voice and Sing" (LBW, PH, TPH, UMH)

"O God of Love, O King of Peace" (HB, HUCC, LBW, PH, TPH)

"O God, We Bear the Imprint of Your Face" (TPH)

"Where Charity and Love Prevail" (LBW, UMH, WB)

22

RUTH AND NAOMI

(Ordinary Time)

INTRODUCTION

Friendship is the focus of this worship service — specifically the friendship of two women. It might be a very interesting service to experience with a youth group; perhaps the story of David and Jonathan could be used as a companion piece so that teenagers of both genders could relate to the various characters.

Two women — three, really — transcended ancient tradition and took their place as our foremothers of faith. Parable women, who pulled the rug out from under the feet of tradition — who looked into each others' eyes and knew there must be mercy for them in the heart of this ancient granite God, even as they adopted a way of life unacceptable in the teachings of their culture. They were daughters of that culture, whose courage to live by their own heart and wits began to transform the world and their own lives.

Naomi. "No, call me Bitter," she said. But not too bitter to set aside the old command and to care for her foreign daughters-in-law. The bond among them crossed racial lines and broke immovable fences of prejudice.

Ruth. Standing at the border of Moab, with the brook Zered at her back, glancing one last time at the beckoning mountains of home ... with the persuasive reasoning of Naomi begging her to return to a life that might yet *be* a life.

In that instant, the spirit of the One yet to be born stirs within time; as Ruth replies, "Entreat me not to leave you ..." and the mother-in-law becomes sister; ancient enemies are reconciled; and she who has no future, under law, takes her destiny into her own hands and thus gives it to God.

In a culture that has pitted women against one another for the attention and protection of men, we discover a biblical model of two women who have bonded with each other; and the hand that Ruth extends grips a *woman's* hand.

In place of abandonment, God called forth a new and parable-like bond.

Ruth, who shares Naomi's emptiness, becomes the great-grandmother of David, the ancestor of Jesus, so that our Messiah, our brother is born in the lineage of one who assumed another's hopelessness.

Ruth, companion on our journey, walk among us now.

—Gail Ricciuti, from "Partners in Parable"[1]

PREPARATION

The room arrangement should facilitate small-group discussion.

❀

GATHERING

Leader: Unless God builds the house,

People: those who build it labor in vain.

Leader: Unless God watches over the city,

People: the watcher stays awake in vain.

Leader: It is in vain that you rise up early
and go late to rest,
eating the bread of anxious toil;
for God gives sleep to God's beloved.

—Psalm 127:1–2

PRAYER/POEM OF CONFESSION (unison)

O God, our Father and Mother,
we confess today that your own sons and daughters in Christ
have let you down.
Dominated by our fears,
we have trampled and smothered one another.
We have smothered the tenderness of man;
we have smothered the creative thinking of women.
Help women to discover honest and life-giving relationships;
help men to open their hearts to each other in friendship;
help us to create a community of brothers and sisters,
where we can live with each
other in creative community
   man with man
   woman with woman
   man with woman. Amen.

—Kerstin Lindqvist, Ulla Bardh[2]

**RECEIVING FORGIVENESS FROM GOD
AND THE PEACE OF CHRIST FROM EACH OTHER**

Leader: We know that nothing can seperate us from the love of
God in Christ Jesus.

People: We receive God's grace and Christ's peace to live again.

Leader: Let us share with one another the grace and peace we have
received.

SONG

"If the Lord Does Not Build," Dan Schutte[3]

I. RUTH AND NAOMI:
THE STORY THUS FAR...

SCRIPTURE

Ruth 1:11–18

REFLECTION AND SHARING

- Who was your first friend?

  - For women, a first female friend.

  - For men, a first male friend.

- Describe the person and a memory of that friendship.

- What does friendship mean to you?

*After a time of discussion the worship leader calls the group back together and
moves on to Part II.*

II. RUTH AND NAOMI:
THE FRIENDSHIP CONTINUES...

SCRIPTURE

Ruth 4:7–17

REFLECTIONS BY WORSHIP LEADER ON THE SCRIPTURE

BECOMING NEW FRIENDS

Response in small groups or by entire group.

PRAYER (unison)

Yahweh, God of Israel,
As Ruth loved Naomi,
   so may I love those with whom I join myself.
As Ruth left the house of her parents,
   the land of her birth to companion a beloved one,
   so may I journey faithfully in the company of my loved ones.
As Ruth spoke her troth to Naomi,
   so may I never withhold words of loving.
As Ruth worked with strength in the harvest,
   so may I work in your vineyard.
As Ruth trusted in you,
   so may I trust.
As Ruth listened to Naomi, her kinswoman,
   so may I listen to those who would impart wisdom to me.
As Ruth went out with boldness to redeem her family according to
   the custom,
   so would I leave behind timidity and be a woman who claims
   redemption for Israel.
As Ruth received the blessing of those who witnessed her,
   so would I be blessed by my people.
As Ruth built up the House of Israel like Rachel and like Leah,
   so would I build this House in this time.

—Ann Johnson[4]

SONG

"No Longer Strangers," Avery and Marsh[5]

CLOSING (unison)

O God, whom to follow
is to risk our whole lives;
as Ruth and Naomi
loved and held to one another,
abandoning the ways of the past,
so may we also not be divided,
but travel together
into that strange land where you will
lead us through Jesus Christ. Amen.

—Janet Morley[6]

NOTES

1. Excerpt from "Partners in Parable," sermon preached by Rev. Gail Ricciuti, Celebrate Women Conference Synod of the Northeast, 1981.

2. Prayer/Poem of Confession excerpted from "Accept Our Deep Longing to Live" by Kerstin Lindqvist and Ulla Bardh. Reproduced with permission from *No Longer Strangers,* © 1983 WCC Publications, World Council of Churches, 150 route de Ferney, 1211 Geneva 2, Switzerland.

3. "If the Lord Does Not Build" by Dan Schutte, S.J. © 1975 North American Liturgy Resources, 2110 W. Peoria Ave., Phoenix, AZ 85029. As found in *Glory and Praise* by the same publisher.

4. Unison Prayer by Ann Johnson from *Miryam of Nazareth,* © 1984 by Ave Maria Press, Notre Dame, IN 46556. Used with permission of publisher.

5. "No Longer Strangers," by Avery and Marsh from *Songbook #8,* published by Proclamation Productions, Inc., Orange Square, Port Jervis, NY 12771.

6. Closing Prayer by Janet Morley from *All Desires Known,* © 1988 by Morehouse-Barlow, 78 Danbury Road, Wilton, CT 06897.

SUGGESTED ALTERNATE HYMNS

"Blest Be the Tie That Binds" (HB, LBW, MH, PH, TPH, UMH)

"Give to the Winds Thy Fears" (HB, MH, PH, TPH, UMH, WB)

"God of Our Life" (HB, MH, PH, TPH, WB)

"Great Is Thy Faithfulness" (TPH, UMH)

"We Need Each Other's Voice to Sing" (NHLC)

"We Travel toward a Land Unknown" (NHLC)

23

SPEAKING THE GOSPEL TO THE POWERFUL

(Ordinary Time)

INTRODUCTION

Nothing makes many mainline churches (Protestant and Catholic alike) more nervous than the word "evangelism." It carries for us negative connotations of pressure tactics or judgmentalism; and many of us would rather be on the clean-up crew or even serve a stint on the *stewardship* campaign than join the evangelism committee! Yet we call ourselves "evangelical," when we are able to remember and claim the roots of the word from the ancient Greek: *evangelion* — good news.

The comedian Stan Freeberg, in cooperation with the National Council of Churches, has produced a series of thirty-second radio "spots" created for use by local ecumenical councils. Their purpose was reaching out to unchurched listeners with a humorous but thought-provoking invitation to consider faith in contemporary life. This service uses a number of those audio vignettes to help the church community *itself* take thought regarding old assumptions and prejudicial beliefs that impact the way we offer the news of Christ's love to people in today's world.

PREPARATION

The worship area is best arranged with chairs arranged in a triangle so all are facing each other. One side of the triangle has chairs for each of the role-players from the list below.

Prior to the service, cards must be prepared assigning the following roles (or others like them) that can be handed to specific volunteers during the service. It is probable that time will not permit a group to use all of the characters listed below. In that case, leaders should select those that seem most relevant to their community, perhaps three to five in number:

- City Council Member
- State Supreme Court Judge
- State Representative

- Police Sergeant
- Hospital Administrator
- Junior Vice President of a Major Corporation
- Armed Services Officer
- School Board Member

❋

CALL TO WORSHIP: "What a Concept!"[1]

The taped vignette is amplified over a sound system.

SINGING

"We Have This Ministry," Jim Strathdee, in *Everflowing Streams*

PRAYER OF CONFESSION: "The Golf Date"

SHARING THE GOOD NEWS

... this way?

Here is printed in the order of worship a rectangular box, "tract"-size, within which elaborate lettering announces, "Have you heard of the FIVE CALVINIST LAWS?" Beneath this graphic appears a large hand emerging from a cloud, index finger pointing at a small Ziggy-type figure who in turn is pointing at himself, asking "Who ... Me?" Above this design are the words "Law 1: You are totally depraved."

... or this way? Acts 8:26–40 (ILL)

An angel said to Philip, "Rise and go toward the south to the road that goes down from Jerusalem to Gaza." This is a desert road. And Philip rose and went. And behold, an Ethiopian, a eunuch, a minister of the Candace, queen of the Ethiopians, in charge of all her treasure, had come to Jerusalem to worship and was returning; seated in his chariot, the Ethiopian was reading the prophet Isaiah. And the Spirit said to Philip, "Go up and join this chariot." So Philip hurried over to the Ethiopian, and heard him reading Isaiah the prophet, and asked, "Do you understand what you are reading?" And the Ethiopian replied, "How can I, unless someone guides me?" And he invited Philip to come up and sit with him.
    Now the passage of the Scripture which he was reading was this:

> As a sheep led to the slaughter
> or a lamb before its shearer is dumb,
> so this one does not say a word.

> In the humiliation of the silent one,
> justice was denied.
> Who can describe the generation
> of the one whose life is taken up from the earth?

And the Ethiopian eunuch said to Philip, "About whom, pray, does the prophet say this, about himself or about someone else?" Then Philip opened his mouth, and beginning with this Scripture, told the Ethiopian the good news of Jesus. And as they went along the road they came to some water, and the eunuch said, "See, here is water! What is to prevent my being baptized?" And he commanded the chariot to stop, and they both went down into the water, Philip and the eunuch, and Philip baptized him. And when they came up out of the water, the Spirit of the Sovereign caught up Philip; and the Ethiopian eunuch saw him no more, and went on his way rejoicing. But Philip was found at Azotus, and passing on he preached the gospel to all the towns till he came to Caesarea.

SOLO

"Pass It On," *The Methodist Hymnal*

After the reading and solo, the leader should explain briefly the significance of the eunuch as a government official of the time and use the following questions — either printed in the order of worship, or asked verbally — as a springboard into discussion:

- Which is more significant to the message of the story: that the Ethiopian was physically altered or that he held power and prestige?

- What insights do you have on Philip's approach to "evangelism"?

- The story seems to indicate that no matter who embraces the gospel, or how different from ourselves they are, their embrace of it is to be honored and respected. Is this consistent with your theology and with your experience as a member of the church?

- The Ethiopian eunuch was not only a foreigner, but was one of "those people" who were barred by religious law from being a full participant in the community. Most major denominations still — to our great shame — have restrictions against fully welcoming certain groups of people as fellow believers: notably, gay and lesbian Christians (by our doctrine and our heterosexism) and differently abled persons (by our church architecture and our own dis-ease). Discuss whether, in your opinion, Philip felt any conflict in conversing with or subsequently in baptizing the official, and what you think the vignette has to say to the contemporary Church.

HOW DO YOU SPEAK THE GOSPEL TO POWER?

"Changes"

"Life in the Fast Lane"

After the tapes are heard (and when the laughter dies down!), those with assigned "roles" (see the Preparation explanation of role cards) take seats in the row of chairs facing the congregation and proceed to describe themselves. Worshippers (as a body) are then invited to engage in conversation with each one, determining how they would open a discussion with a person of a particular profession or interest regarding "the good news of Jesus." After a few minutes of this engagement, a crucial "switch" should be explained by the leader, who asks:

"Now: how would your approach change if you suddenly knew this school board member (or corporate executive, etc.) to be gay? Or if this city council member were in a wheelchair?"

COMMITTING OURSELVES

Singing

"I'm Gonna Live So God Can Use Me," African-American Spiritual, *The Presbyterian Hymnal*

Sharing Our Gifts

Concerns of the Church and Prayers

The Final, Evangelical Word: 1 John 4:7–12

Response

"We Are Simply Asked," words by Peter Byrne, S.J., from *Songs of Shalom*[2]

These words may either be spoken or sung by the community.

❦

NOTES

1. "What a Concept!," "The Golf Date," "Changes," and "Life in the Fast Lane" are all found on the audio recording "Come On Back!" by Stan Freeberg, produced by SANDCASTLES, c/o PRTVC, 1727 Clifton Rd., Atlanta, GA 30329.

2. "We Are Simply Asked," words by Peter Byrne, music by Jim Strathdee, from *Songs of Shalom*, © 1983 by the Section on Ministry of the Laity, Board of Discipleship, United Methodist Church, Nashville.

SUGGESTED ALTERNATE HYMNS

"Christ for the World We Sing" (HB, MH, PH, UMH)

"Help Us Accept Each Other" (TPH, UMH)

"Here I Am, Lord" (TPH, UMH)

"Lord, Speak to Me, That I May Speak" (HB, LBW, MH, PH, TPH, UMH)

"Lord, You Give the Great Commission" (UMH)

"Love Divine, All Loves Excelling" (HB, HUCC, LBW, MH, PH, TPH, UMH, WB)

"Thou Whose Purpose Is to Kindle" (HUCC, WB)

24

REFORMATION PEOPLE

(Reformation Sunday)

INTRODUCTION

This service was inspired by "Reformation Women" found in Part I of this book (see pp. 99–106). It is well suited for larger or regional gatherings such as mission consultations, celebrating our rich and varied history as people of faith. With some research the service can easily be adapted to another part of the world or another denomination. It is an excellent way to teach and to learn about church history, while incorporating many participants. As "potters" they too help to mold and shape the life and ministry (and thereby the history) of the church.

PREPARATION

The worship center for this service is a church-like building constructed of clay blocks. (See above p. 99 for more detailed instructions. For a very large group — more than sixty — it might be interesting to build two or three different types of church buildings.)

The various "characters" may speak from their places in the congregation or come to a center microphone. If planning is done well in advance, characters could be in costume.

❧

CALL TO WORSHIP

Leader: I will bless the Lord at all times;
God's praises shall be on my lips continuously;

People: my soul glories in Yahweh,
let the humble hear and rejoice!

Leader: proclaim with me the greatness of Yahweh,
together let us extol God's name.

People: How good God is — only taste and see!
Happy are those who take refuge in God!

—from Psalm 34

PRAYER OF CONFESSION

God of history and of my heart,
so much has happened to me during these whirlwind days:
    We have known death and birth;
    we have been brave and scared;
    we have hurt, we have helped;
    we have been honest, we have lied;
    we have destroyed, we have created;
    we have been with people, we have been lonely;
    we have been loyal, we have betrayed;
    we have decided, we have waffled;
    we have laughed, we have cried.
You know our frail hearts and our frayed history —
and now another day begins.
    O God, help me to believe in beginnings
    and in my beginning again,
    no matter how often I have failed before.

—Ted Loder, *Guerrillas of Grace*[1]

ASSURANCE OF GOD'S PARDON AND
THE PEACE OF CHRIST

Leader: Each time we fall short of what God intends God reaches out to us in Christ and lifts us up again and again.

People: We believe the good news of the gospel: in Jesus Christ we are forgiven.

HYMN

"The Church of Christ in Every Age," *The Presbyterian Hymnal*

SCRIPTURE

Jeremiah 18:1–6

WE CALL UPON A HOST OF WITNESSES[2]

1. John Knox

I AM JOHN KNOX. I was born in 1515 in Scotland. I went to Geneva to study with John Calvin, and while I was there, I organized a church for the English-speaking refugees. I remained in exile for twelve years, whereafter I returned to lead the Reformation in Scotland. When the first General Assembly of Scotland was convened in 1560, I submitted a Confession of Faith, which was adopted by the Scottish parliament. I compiled *The Book of Discipline,* which provided for the government of the church by sessions, synods, and the General Assembly. In addition the book decreed that every congregation was to establish a school for the teaching of Latin, grammar, and the catechism. Most consider that I laid the groundwork for an educated ministry and an equally educated laity.

2. Katherine Zell

See above p.101 for this biography.

> *Response:*   We are Reformation people.
> We affirm our responsibility
> to share the earth's goods with the earth's people,
> to build structures of economic justice for all.

3. John Witherspoon

I AM JOHN WITHERSPOON. I immigrated from Scotland to Princeton, New Jersey, in 1768 to be president of the College of New Jersey. The citizens of New Jersey elected me to the Continental Congress, where I was the only active minister to sign the Declaration of Independence. I served as pastor of the Princeton Presbyterian Church and helped to organize the first General Assembly of the Presbyterian Church.

4. Katherine Jones Bennett

I AM KATHERINE JONES BENNETT. I served as president of the Woman's Board of Home Missions from 1909 to 1923 and then as vice-president of the Presbyterian Board of National Missions. I was from Englewood, New Jersey, and a graduate of Elmira College. In 1916 I was the first woman ever to speak as president of the Woman's Board from the platform at General Assembly. One account of that states "and talk she did — brightly, sprightly, and wittily, much to the point and entirely to the delight of the 900 men who made up her audience." Finally Presbyterian Women had received recognition as an independent agency of the General Assembly. In 1927 Margaret Hodge and I issued a report finding unrest among women dissatisfied with their status and role, and the "benevolent paternalism" of men who granted some voice, but no vote in ecclesiastical matters. Margaret and I made it clear that women wanted a vote in the decision-making bodies of the church. Our report led to a special Conference of Women in 1929 and the eventual approval of women's ordination as elders in 1930. I was asked to pray before the vote for a national organization of women and included these words: "May we quiet our hearts and our minds and come before thee, being willing to be led in the right way. . . . May our spirits be so filled with the cause that we represent and with the people whose future may be influenced by those things that are done here today that we may put aside smaller issues."

> *Response:*   We are Reformation people.
> We are healers and holy, priests and prophets.

We affirm our responsibility to break bread
and lift a cup in the name of liberation.

5. James W. C. Pennington

I AM JAMES W. C. PENNINGTON. I was pastor of the First Colored Presbyterian Church in New York City from 1848 to 1856. I visited Europe three
times to lecture on slavery and received an honorary degree from the University of Heidelberg. I wrote the story of my life in *The Fugitive Blacksmith*
and *Text Book of the Origin, and History... of the Colored People*, in which I
tried to refute prejudices and misconceptions about Negroes.

6. Marguerite Kellis

I AM MARGUERITE KELLIS, a member of the Shinnecock Indian Tribe and
a weaver of baskets. I used my knowledge of the healing properties of roots
and berries and my skill in the healing arts to bring comfort to the elderly
and the dying as well as serving as midwife for the births of many Shinnecock babies. My husband and I gathered willows and berries for coloring
the baskets in red, purple, and lavender. My family called me the "rock-
bound coast of Maine," like a great boulder weathered by many storms
but remaining constant. I lived into my eighties and am very proud of my
niece Elizabeth Haile, the first Native American clergywoman ordained in
the Presbyterian Church.

> *Response:* We are Reformation people.
> We are moral agents who make decisions
> about our bodies.
> We affirm our responsibility to make choices
> that promote dignity and reflect love.

7. Edler G. Hawkins

I AM EDLER G. HAWKINS, founder and pastor of St. Augustine Pres-
byterian Church in the Bronx and past president of the Afro-American
Presbyterian Council of the North and West. I educated Eugene Carson
Blake so that he could help to launch the Commission on Religion and
Race in 1963. In 1964 I was elected as the first black moderator of the
General Assembly. Gayraud Wilmore described me as always dignified but
irrepressible. I spent much of my life holding in tension the twin goals of
black cultural identity and interracial integration.

8. Lilian Hert Alexander

I AM LILIAN HERT ALEXANDER. I was a longtime member and elder of
Third Presbyterian Church in Rochester, New York. Throughout my life
I was actively involved in addressing human needs and in expanding the
role of women in society. In college I was involved in the women's suffrage
movement in the early 1900s. When our group was banned from meeting

on campus, we moved our meetings to a nearby cemetery. I was the mother of five when I was active in my church. In the 1940s I became a member of the Nominating Committee of Session. At the first meeting I asked why there were no women on the Session. You could hear their jaws drop; they couldn't believe what they had heard; how could this nice meeting be so rudely interrupted. I convinced the Session in 1953 and then the Presbytery to overture the General Assembly for the ordination of women to the ministry. It finally happened in 1956. I was honored in 1985 to receive a Women of Faith award at the Women's Breakfast at General Assembly.

9. Lin Yutang

I AM LIN YUTANG. I was born in China to Christian parents and educated at Christian Schools, but renounced my faith and became an ardent Confucianist. I studied at Harvard and in Germany. I served as head of the Arts and Letters Division of UNESCO. I was considered a scholar and invented a Chinese typewriter. During the last decade of my life I lived in New York City. My wife persuaded me to attend her church, Madison Avenue Presbyterian. I returned again and again to that church to study the awe-inspiring simplicity and beauty of the teachings of Jesus. I wrote about my experience in an article "Why I Came Back to Christianity" in *Presbyterian Life* in 1959: "The scales began to fall from my eyes. I am an orphan no longer. Where I had been drifting I have arrived. The Sunday morning when I joined the Christian Church was a homecoming."

> *Response:*   We are Reformation people.
> We are voters and change agents.
> We affirm our responsibility
> to influence public policy
> and to build a new world,
> starting with the struggling poor.

HYMN

"Come, Great God of All the Ages," *The Presbyterian Hymnal*

PARTICIPATING IN A RE-FORMATION: CREATING OUR OWN NINETY-FIVE THESES AND "POSTING THEM"

See above p. 104.

A LITANY OF THE SAINTS

> *Leader:*   God our Creator, we praise you for the saints:
> for saints who have gone before us;
> for saints who are alive today;
> for saints who are in our midst;
> for the sainthood in us all.

Right side: God of Love,
we thank you for saints who have loved us —
for families through whom we were created,
the people who first loved us and taught us of your love:

Left side: For relatives and friends who responded to our needs;
for relatives and friends who needed our love.

Right side: For matriarchs, patriarchs, prophets, and priests;
for disciples, apostles, leaders, and servants.

Left side: For pastors and missionaries, deacons and elders;
For educators and healers, clerks and cooks.
God, to whom we come in faith,
we thank you for the faith of the saints:

Right side: For Abraham and Sarah, Mary and Joseph;
For Hannah and Elijah, Elizabeth and John.

Left side: For Elijah Parish Lovejoy and Mary Slessor,
Marcus and Narcissa Whitman.

Right side: For Martin Luther and Teresa of Avila,
John Calvin and Margaret of Navarre.

Left side: God, whose forgiveness brings us hope,
we remember the saints who experienced hope:

Right side: Jacob and Samuel, Ruth and Naomi,
Augustine and Donaldina Cameron;

Left side: Kagawa, Schweitzer, and Jane Woolsey.

Right side: God, who wants justice and peace in the world,
we honor saints whose peaceful ways
give us a vision of your realm:

Left side: Archbishop Romero and Bishop Tutu, Maura Clarke,
Ita Ford, Dorothy Kazel, and Jean Donovan;

Right side: Gandhi and Sojourner Truth,
Martin Luther King and Rosa Parks,

Left side: Dietrich Bonhoeffer and John Conner.

Leader: God, we are renewed by the courage of the saints of history. We are inspired by the saints who walk among us today. May your Spirit move each of us to be teachers, healers, preachers, and peacemakers in the world. May we join the great cloud of witnesses in faith.

All: As the saints have heard your call and claimed their faith,
          may we also hear your call and respond faithfully.

                                                —John Holtzclaw, Rosemary C. Mitchell

BENEDICTION

✸

NOTES

1. The Prayer of Confession is by Ted Loder from *Guerrillas of Grace*, © 1984 by LuraMedia, Inc., San Diego, CA 92121. Used by permission of publisher.

2. The words for "We Call Upon a Host of Witnesses" were written by Rosemary C. Mitchell, using historical information drawn from *American Presbyterians: A Pictorial History* by James H. Smylie, *Our Presbyterian Heritage* by Paul Carlson, *The Presbyterian Predicament* by M. Coalter, J. Mulder, and L. Weeks, *Conversions* by H. Kerr and J. Mulder, *Women of the Reformation* by Roland Bainton, and *A Sampler of Saints* by Elizabeth Verdesi and Sylvia Thorsen-Smith.

SUGGESTED ALTERNATE HYMNS

"Have Thine Own Way, Lord" (HB, HUCC, MH, UMH)

"I Love to Tell the Story" (HB, HUCC, MH, PH, UMH)

"Rise Up, O Saints of God" (LBW)

"Through the Night of Doubt and Sorrow" (HB, HUCC, LBW)

"Today We All Are Called to Be Disciples" (TPH)

"We All Are One in Mission" (TPH)

"When There Is No Star to Guide You" (NHLC)